BLANK PAGE

First Printing
March 2018

LEARNING TO LEAD: Converting the Heart
The Five Verbs of Saving Faith

ISBN: 978-0-9993545-5-1

List Price: **$15.95 each**
plus postage and handling

Additional copies can be obtained from:

Disciple Maker Ministries
905 Golf Course Road N.W.
Hutchinson, MN 55350

612-750-5515

LanceKetchum@msn.com
www.disciplemakerministries.org

Published by:
The Old Paths Publications, Inc.
Email: TOP@theoldpathspublications.com
Website: www.theoldpathspublications.com

IN APPRECIATION

A special THANK YOU to the members and friends of Shepherd's Fold Baptist Church of Hutchinson, Minnesota for their patience with me in the unfolding and development of the truths contained in this book. You have helped me to grow through these studies. God blessed in the many decisions that you made to the glory of God during the preaching of this series. It has also been a blessing to see the increase of spiritual fruit through your lives as you began to implement the doctrine of Grace into the practice of your everyday lives. Praise God for many of you who have come to receive the gift of God's salvation through the preaching and teaching of the truths of God's wondrous Gospel.

I also want to thank Mrs. Julie Rydberg for her careful and meticulous proofreading of the manuscript. I pray our Lord will bless you in a special way for your generosity in giving many hours to this work.

To my wife, Patty – thank you for your patience in allowing me almost every free moment of our lives together for the last two years to finish this work. You catered to my every need to allow me the time I needed. Your graciousness has exemplified all the truths defined by the doctrine of Grace. Your self-sacrificing love reveals the selflessness that manifests the Spirit-filled life. You are undoubtedly a living definition exemplifying the word "helpmeet."

Table of Contents

Preface

By the late 1600's, liberal theological thought began a steady slide into apostasy when a reductionist philosophical notion known as *pluralism* came into religious circles. *Pluralism* is the teaching that says it really does not matter *what* you believe about God, as long as you believe in *God* or **a** *god* in some form.

Pluralism denotes any metaphysical theory claiming that reality consists of a multiplicity of distinct, fundamental entities. The term was first used by Christian Wolff (1679-1754), and later popularized by William James in *The Will to Believe* (1896). As a theological term, it refers to the belief that "god" exists with many different names and within all *religions*. These *religions* worship the same "god," only using different names and belief systems. These are commonly referred to as different *faiths*.

For this type of theological reductionism, Pluralism taught that *doctrine* (the teachings of various religions) is secondary (sometimes totally irrelevant) to "belief" in a *god*, whatever the form or practice that belief system takes. Communion between various *faiths* is based upon any ground of commonality while ignoring their doctrinal differences. In most cases, the only ground of commonality these *faiths* possess is belief in a *god* of some kind. Pluralism became the basis for *Ecumenicism.* Pluralism was based upon a religious philosophy of reducing theological requirements for salvation to the simplest common denominator; i.e., belief in a *god*, regardless of what this *god* was called.

Pluralism became the norm for those trained in classical Theological institutions (which were more *philosophical* than *theological*). Pluralism was merely one step away from Universalism. Classical theological education led to both Higher and Lower Criticism and, ultimately, to the theological liberalism of the early 1900's.

Mohandas Karamchand Gandhi (who came to be known merely as Mahatma Gandhi, 1869-1948) was very influential in establishing Pluralism within Ecumenicism and the present-day *anathema* about proselytizing those of other *faiths*. Eastern Mystic religions such as Buddhism, Hinduism, and Manchurian Gnosticism, and many theological liberals were being greatly influenced during the late 1800's and early 1900's. Gandhi is quoted as saying[1]:

> After long study and experience, I have come to the conclusion that (1) all religions are true; (2) all religions have some error in them; (3) all religions are almost as dear to me as my own Hinduism, in as much as all human beings should be as dear to one as one's own close relatives. My own veneration for other faiths is the same as that for my own faith; therefore no thought of conversion is possible. (underling added)

Although fundamental Christianity (and most of Evangelical Christianity) rejected both Pluralism and its illegitimate *child* called Ecumenicism, those declaring themselves *New Evangelicals* and holding to a Universalist Ecclesiology (*not the same as Universalist Soteriology*), began to *dialog* with the Liberals, arguing about seeking to maintain theological and cultural *relevancy* within the Christian *community.* This pursuit of *relevancy* by New Evangelicals has been the cause of their continuing and gradual compromise of truth. Because of this *dialog,* most of the participants began to try to find the most reducible form of the *Gospel* to which they could agree to have a degree of *unity.* This *Soteriological Reductionism* came forth in three main streams within Evangelicalism and Fundamentalism by the 1950's:

1. Easy Believism (New Evangelicalism)
2. Only Believism (Evangelicalism)
3. Easy Prayerism (much of Fundamentalism; *One, Two, Three, say it after me!*)

Paul's message in Galatians 1:6-9 is clear: **If the Gospel can be perverted in any way, evangelism is perverted as well as the necessary faith that brings genuine salvation and conversion.** These three forms of Soteriological Reductionism

---

[1] M. K. Gandhi, ***All Men Are Brothers: Life and Thoughts of Mahatma Gandhi as Told in His Own Words***, (Paris, UNESCO 1958), 60.

have filled evangelical local churches with people masquerading as "born again" Christians when in reality, most of them are nothing more than "whited sepulchers." This reality exists because all three forms of Reductionism are perversions in varying degrees of the Gospel of Jesus Christ.

Easy Believism (New Evangelicalism)

Easy Believism was the most extreme form of Reductionism within Evangelicalism emerging out this era. The *common denominator* within Easy Believism was that Jesus was the Son of God incarnate and that He died for the sins of mankind. If a person believed these basic truths about Jesus, regardless of any false beliefs to which he might hold, he could still claim to be "born again." It most cases, few, if any, of the objective and definitive facts of the Gospel were required to be taught or understood before a salvation decision could be made.

Iain Murray, in *Revivals and Revivalism*[2], says that the Presbyterian Evangelist Charles Finney (1792-1875) "believed that all that was needed for conversion was a resolution signified by standing, kneeling, or coming forward, and because the Holy Spirit always acts when a sinner acts, the public resolution could be treated as 'identical with the miraculous inward change of sudden conversion'."

Easy Believism has four basic tenets:

1. A conversion *experience* is the *only* thing necessary for genuine salvation (whatever defines that *experience*). If a person can testify to a time he *accepted/received* Christ *into his heart*, that person has eternal security and should be given assurance of salvation. Therefore, a testimony of such an *experience* was sought to give *assurance* that salvation had taken place. Many types of *experiences* are accepted for this assurance.

---

[2] Ian Murray, **Revivals and Revivalism: The Making and Marring of American Evangelicalism**, (Edinburgh: Banner of Truth, 1994).

2. There are no rules or standards expected within the Christian life after one was saved. Anyone saying that such things existed *under grace* was a *legalist.*
3. Once saved and having received the Holy Spirit, the Christian is at *liberty* to make decisions according to the Holy Spirit's leading of his conscience. The Word of God is not the *only way* God directs believers to His will. *Dogmatic applications* of doctrine should be avoided and *personal liberty* should be allowed free expression.
4. Not every Christian will live a godly life, therefore the genuineness of his conversion should not be *judged* by outward circumstances or by external evidences of habitual carnality.

Only Believism (Evangelicalism)

Although Only Believism is less Reductionism than Easy Believism, it is equally perverting. Only Believism reduces the the believer's *response to Gospel* to *only* believing. In other words, all responses to obey the Gospel (Romans 10:16) such as repentance, receiving, confessing, and calling upon the name of Jesus are all the *same as*, and are encapsulated in *only believing.* These various responses are not individual acts and are all merely *aspects* of believing that need not be expressed individually.

All the other verbs describe *aspects* of a salvation decision, but these *aspects* cannot be reduced to *only believing.* In other words, repenting of sin (Luke 24:7) and "dead works" (Hebrews 6:1), understanding (Matthew 13:23), believing the objective facts of the Gospel of Jesus Christ (Acts 8:37; 16:31-32), publicly confessing one's belief that Jesus is Jehovah (Romans 10:9; "LORD," see Joel 2:32), calling on the name of Jesus to save (Romans 10:13), and receiving the indwelling of the Holy Spirit (John 1:12) are all aspects of a proper response to the Gospel in a genuine salvation decision and should be explained in the presentation of the Gospel of Jesus Christ. True Evangelism involves both the explanation of the objective facts of the Gospel and the objective required responses to the Gospel in order for true, supernatural "conversion" to be created. This is exemplified in Paul's dealing with the Philippian jailer and his household.

> [27] And the keeper of the prison awaking out of his sleep, and seeing the prison doors open, he drew out his sword, and would have killed himself, supposing that the prisoners had been fled. [28] But Paul cried with a loud voice, saying, Do thyself no harm: for we are all here. [29] Then he called for a light, and sprang in, and came trembling, and fell down before Paul and Silas, [30] And brought them out, and said, Sirs, what must I do to be saved? [31] And they said, Believe on the Lord Jesus Christ, and thou shalt be saved, and thy house. [32] And they spake unto him the word of the Lord, and to all that were in his house. [33] And he took them the same hour of the night, and washed *their* stripes; and was baptized, he and all his, straightway. [34] And when he had brought them into his house, he set meat before them, and rejoiced, believing in God with all his house (Acts 16:27-34).

Only Believists would stop at Acts 16:31. However, verse 32 clearly states, "And they spake unto him the word of the Lord, and to all that were in his house." In other words, there was a thorough explanation of the Gospel, the necessary responses to the Gospel involved in a faith decision, and even the expectations of a believer once that believer trusted Christ for salvation. We know this latter fact because the Philippian jailer and "all that were in his house" believed and were "baptized." Aquila and Priscilla did this same thing with a man named Apollos (Acts 18:24-28).

Only Believism did not reduce the necessary *objective facts* of the Gospel to the degree Easy Believism did. Only Believism reduced the necessary *responses* to those objective facts of the Gospel to *only believing*.

Easy Prayerism (much of Fundamentalism)

This has come to be known as *One, Two, Three, say it after me!* In this evangelism methodology the evangelists gives a quick *run through* the Gospel (five or six verses called the *Roman's Road*). The person is asked if he understands and believes he is a sinner, understands and believes he needs to be saved, and if he is willing to pray and ask God to save him. If the sinner says the

Sinner's Prayer (*repeat these words after me*), he is told he is eternally saved and given assurance of salvation.

Those instructed in this methodology are told to avoid any discussion outside of the few verses in the *Roman's Road* and move the person as quickly as possible to *praying the prayer.* Everything else can be dealt with after *praying the prayer* and *getting saved.*

This methodology got a lot of people to *walk the isles*, get baptized, and join local churches. However, the biggest task was keeping more *coming in the front door than were going out the backdoor* because most these people made only quasi and pseudo salvation decisions. This is what Christ dealt with in the parable of the Sower and the Soils (Matthew 13:1-23; take careful note of the word "understandeth" in verses 19 and 23).

There MUST BE clear understanding of the objective facts of the Gospel *and* the objective required verb responses to the Gospel before conversion can take place in the heart (Matthew 13:15).

The Crossless Gospel

The *Crossless Gospel* is a merging of various aspects all three of these forms of Soteriological Reductionism. The three basic tenets of the *Crossless Gos*pel are:

1. The only fact necessary to faith is a belief in the *historical Jesus*. In other words, believing He is God, or any of the other objective facts of the Gospel are not necessary to either understand or believe in order to believe in Jesus and be saved. This is as close to Universalism as possible.
2. Therefore, only belief in Jesus is necessary to the Gospel proclamation.
3. Easy Prayerism is taken to a whole new level. The person must just believe in Jesus. He does not need to even ask God to save him. A *mental acquiescence* to the historical Jesus is all that is necessary. This *mental acquiescence* need not be expressed in any tangible, empirical, or external way.

Chapter One

Five Verbs of Salvation

UNDERSTANDING

Matthew chapter thirteen is one of the most significant teachings of Jesus in the Gospels because it is in these three parables that He teaches who will be part of the "Kingdom of heaven." The first parable reveals who will be part of the "Kingdom of heaven." It defines the essentials to a genuine *conversion* experience and what is involved in *understanding with the heart* (Matthew 13:15).

> 1 The same day went Jesus out of the house, and sat by the
> sea side. 2 And great multitudes were gathered together unto
> him, so that he went into a ship, and sat; and the whole
> multitude stood on the shore. 3 And he spake many things
> unto **them in parables**, saying, Behold, a sower went forth
> to sow; 4 And when he sowed, some *seeds* fell by the way
> side, and the fowls came and devoured them up: 5 Some fell
> upon stony places, where they had not much earth: and
> forthwith they sprung up, because they had no deepness of
> earth: 6 And when the sun was up, they were scorched; and
> because they had no root, they withered away. 7 And some
> fell among thorns; and the thorns sprung up, and choked
> them: 8 But other fell into good ground, and brought forth
> fruit, some an hundredfold, some sixtyfold, some thirtyfold.
> 9 **Who hath ears to hear, let him hear** (Matthew 13:1-9).

The Gospel of Jesus Christ gives the believer God's specific instructions for responding to the Gospel message in order to receive God's gift of salvation. **The believer must first *understand* what each aspect of Christ's death, burial, and resurrection accomplishes in His work of redemption and THEN respond according to God's specifications of faith in five verbs.**

There are three essential elements within the parable of the *Sower and the Soils* that must work together before a sinner can be brought to the conviction of sin, understand the Gospel, and be "born again" . . . "by grace through faith."

1. The "seed" is the Gospel of Jesus Christ with the specific, objective facts **detailing what Christ has accomplished** for sinners through His death, burial, and resurrection/glorification. These facts MUST BE UNDERSTOOD!
2. The "Sower" is the Holy Spirit of God Who works to illuminate (give understanding to) the Gospel to the sinner's heart. The Holy Spirit works in *synergism* (partnership) with the Spirit-filled soul-winner as he preaches and explains the details of the Gospel (illumination can also happen as the sinner *reads* the Scriptures).
3. The various "soils" are primarily the various *conditions of the hearts* of those in whom the *seed* is being sown. The *conditions of the heart* define the *heart's* relationship to various worldly influences.

Preparing the heart to receive the "seed" is perhaps the greatest essential to a genuine conversion experience. Therefore, the Apostle Paul uses almost three full chapters of his Epistle to the Romans to explain the doctrine of condemnation BEFORE he begins to explain the doctrine of salvation. This is preparing the "soil" of the heart for conversion. The sinner must understand the holiness of God and the sinfulness of sin. *Preparing the heart* is picking up the rocks that hardened a person to their sin and harden a person to the work of the Holy Spirit. Preparing the heart is clearing away the thorns and thistles of worldly ambitions that will grow and choke away any possibility for new life to generate to fruition in the heart.

Preparing the heart to receive the "seed" is what biblical repentance is all about. Many have come to think that repentance is merely an intellect change of the mind about sin, worldliness, and false doctrine. Genuine repentance effects the **mind** (how we think about sin, worldliness, and false doctrine), the **emotions** (how we feel about sin, worldliness, and false doctrine), and **practice** (how we live what we know or believe).

Changing practice is the outcome of genuine repentance and is progressive towards godliness AFTER CONVERSION due to numerous volitional choices. In other words, the way we live our lives **should** progressively be changed by varying degrees as we *grow* to know the Word of God and the God of the Word. However**, until** there is a change of mind that *agrees* with the revealed will of God AND a change of heart that *feels* about sin, worldliness, and false doctrine that corresponds with the way God feels about sin, worldliness, and false doctrine, **repentance is not happening**.

There are varying degrees of this failure revealed in the parable of the Seed and the Soils. **The central focus is that improperly prepared minds and improperly prepared hearts will result in false conversions due to failure to understand what the Gospel of Jesus Christ accomplishes on the sinner's behalf. False conversions are equally probable without preparation of the sinner's heart through biblical repentance.** Just rushing sinners through the *Romans Road* to get them to *pray the prayer* is a gross injustice against God's redemption.

Parables are simple examples and are not always perfect examples. Parables seek to explain very deep spiritual truths by using common physical examples. These physical illustrations can never fully convey the full depth of the spiritual truth they seek to explain.

> 18 Hear ye therefore the parable of the sower. 19 When any
> one heareth the word of the kingdom, and **understandeth *it***
> **not**, then cometh the wicked *one*, and catcheth away that
> which was sown in his heart. This is he which received seed
> by the way side. 20 But he that received the seed into stony
> places, the same is he that heareth the word, and anon with
> joy receiveth it; 21 Yet hath he not root in himself {*no depth*
> *of understanding*}, but dureth for a while: for when
> tribulation or persecution ariseth because of the word, by and
> by he is offended. 22 He also that received seed among the
> thorns is he that heareth the word; and the care of this world,
> and the deceitfulness of riches, choke the word, and he
> becometh unfruitful. 23 But he that received seed into the
> good ground is he that heareth the word, and **understandeth**

it; which also beareth fruit, and bringeth forth, some an hundredfold, some sixty, some thirty (Matthew 13:18-23).

In other words, inward transformation/regeneration can never take place without this *understanding*. **The critical detail here is that *understanding* with the head must become *understanding* with the heart before saving faith is produced through the operations of the Holy Spirit of God (i.e., germination of the Seed or regeneration).** The proper response to the Gospel is what defines *believing*, or what is more commonly referred to as *saving faith*.

The first verb in a faith decision to be "born again" is the verb REPENT. There MUST be repentance of sin (Romans 1:18-32). There MUST be repentance of one's trust in his own moralism (Romans 2:1-29). There MUST be repentance of one's trust in sacramental rituals as means of conferring the grace of God in salvation (Romans 3:1-20). Perhaps the simplest way to explain repentance is that genuine repentance is *birthed* out of the knowledge of two basic Bible truths. If we want true Bible repentance produced in our lives, we must understand these two basic Bible truths and pursue that understanding from the revelation of God's Word.

1. We must understand how vile and disgusting our sinfulness is in the eyes of God.
2. We must understand the holiness and sanctity of God.

[10] As it is written, There is **none** righteous, no, **not one**: [11]
There is **none** that understandeth, there is **none** that seeketh
after God. [12] They are **all** gone out of the way, they are
together become unprofitable; there is **none** that doeth
good, no, **not one.** [13] Their throat *is* an open sepulchre; with
their tongues they have used deceit; the poison of asps *is*
under their lips: [14] Whose mouth *is* full of cursing and
bitterness: [15] Their feet *are* swift to shed blood: [16]
Destruction and misery *are* in their ways: [17] And the way of
peace have they not known: [18] There is no fear of God before
their eyes (Romans 3:10-18).

Until you see yourself the way God sees you, you will never repent the way God expects you to repent! Genuine repentance sees ourselves just as God sees us. There are no meritorious qualities about us that make us lovely to God or even loveable. We are horrible, wicked, vile, puss-buckets of putridity. God does not love us because we are loveable. God loves us because He is love. Yet, God sees **what we can be** if we get ahold of genuine repentance, get "born again," and begin to live by His enabling grace.

The Greek word *epistrepho* (ep-ee-stref'-o), translated "converted" in Matthew 13:15, literally means *to be turned around.* This "conversion" cannot happen apart from genuine repentance. Repentance is the beginning point of that *turning around.* Peter made this distinction in Acts 3:19; "Repent ye therefore, and be converted, that your sins may be blotted out . . ." Each of the other four verbs in a faith decision also reflect a turning around regarding what we think and believe.

The second verb involved in a faith decision to be "born again" is the verb BELIEVE. Is this just believing in the death, burial, and resurrection of Jesus, or is this believing in what the death, burial, and resurrection of Jesus accomplishes? The word believe reflects a *turning away* from false beliefs about religious "works" (Moralism and Ritualism) so as to believe **solely** in what Christ Jesus accomplished in His death, burial, and resurrection. This *turning away* from "works" is crucial to defining the meaning and practical intent of the word "believe."

To believe the Gospel is to believe **with UNDERSTANDING** what the Gospel accomplishes God-ward in **propitiation** and man-ward in **justification**. To present the Gospel is to present what the Gospel accomplishes first in satisfying God's wrath upon sin (propitiation) and the impartation of God-kind righteousness to the believing sinner in the indwelling Spirit of God (justification).

> [1] Brethren, my heart's desire and prayer to God for Israel is, that they might be saved. [2] For I bear them record that they have a zeal of God, but not according to knowledge {*full discernment or complete understanding*}. [3] For they being ignorant of God's righteousness {*God-kind righteous*ness},

and going about to establish their own righteousness{*man-kind righteousness*}, have not submitted themselves unto the righteousness of God. [4] For Christ *is* the end of the law for righteousness to every one that believeth (Romans 10:1-4).

We can find a *straight-line pattern* in Romans 10:1-13 of God's expectations (responses) to an understanding of the details of the Gospel of Jesus Christ. In Romans 10:9-13, we find three of the five verbs defining a faith decision to be "born again."

1. Believe in thine heart
2. Confess with thine mouth
3. Call on the Name

[9] That if thou shalt confess with thy mouth the Lord Jesus, and shalt believe in thine heart that God hath raised him from the dead, thou shalt be saved. [10] For with the heart man believeth unto righteousness {*imparted*}; and with the mouth confession is made unto salvation. [11] For the scripture saith, Whosoever believeth on him shall not be ashamed. [12]
For there is no difference between the Jew and the Greek: for the same Lord over all is rich unto all that call upon him.
[13] For whosoever shall call upon the name of the Lord shall be saved. [14] How then shall they call on him in whom they have not believed? and how shall they believe in him of whom they have not heard? and how shall they hear without a preacher? [15] And how shall they preach, except they be sent? as it is written, How beautiful are the feet of them that preach the gospel of peace, and bring glad tidings of good things! [16] But they have not all obeyed the gospel. For Esaias saith, Lord, who hath believed our report? [17] So then faith *cometh* by hearing, and hearing by the word of God (Romans 10:1-17).

There is considerable theological depth in the statement of Paul to the question of the Philippian jailer in Acts 16:31 ("Sirs, what must I **do** to be saved?). There Paul says, "believe on the Lord Jesus Christ." Believe is the verb describing the **action** upon the subject "the Lord Jesus Christ." To understand the meaning of the word *believe*, we must return to the Hebrew word *aman* (aw-man'). To *believe* is more than a mere intellectual assent to the facts of the Gospel. The basic idea is to *identify with a certainty*. Therefore, the implication of the word *believe* means *to rest* in the accomplishments of Jesus Christ on our behalf in His finished work of redemption as a *certainty*.

The third verb defining a faith decision to be "born again" is the word CONFESS. Confessing Jesus as LORD dictates the way we receive Him. Confessing Jesus as LORD has more to do with a public announcement or proclamation than it does with a mere assent to Who He is. This was a common practice in ancient times. It was also commonly practiced in certain social circles of yesteryear. For instance, when guests were invited to a ball or large affair, they would enter, hand their invitation with their name and station in life to the servant at the entrance, and their name and station in life would be announced to everyone present. This was to ensure that everyone present knew who they were and that they were to be properly received and treated with the respect and dignity due to their social status in life. In the court of kings, when a dignitary or royalty from another nation or kingdom came as his entourage passed through the crowds, a town crier would publicly announce who it was and what position in life the person held.

Confessing Jesus as LORD certainly would not be considered a private matter. Confessing Jesus as LORD has to do with proclaiming our belief in Who He is before our peers and attaching ourselves to His cause. Confessing Jesus as LORD is a public proclamation of faith in both what Jesus accomplished for sinners through His death, burial, resurrection, and glorification and in Who Jesus is as the incarnate Son of God. He is LORD! To call Jesus LORD means He is the incarnate, eternal, sinless Son of God, Creator of heaven and earth. If Jesus is not LORD, His death, burial, resurrection, and glorification has no merit because He could not fulfill the prophetic proclamations regarding the Promised One beginning with Genesis 3:15. Therefore, His death would merely be the death of another very good, moral prophet of God.

Thus saith the LORD, the King of Israel, and his redeemer,

the LORD of hosts: I am the first, and I am the last, and beside me there is no God (Isaiah 44:6; see also 41:4 and 48:12).

Saying, I am Alpha and Omega, the first and the last; What thou seest, write in a book, and send it unto the seven churches which are in Asia: (Revelation 1:11; see also 1:17; 2:8 and 22:13).

The fourth verb defining a faith decision to be "born again" is the word CALL. This word defines that moment that culminates in the **event** of salvation. Romans 10:13 is a quote from Joel 2:32. Although the truth and application is relevant to all sinners (the intent of the word "whosever"), Paul's instruction in Romans 10:13 is directed primarily to national Israel (Romans 10:1). The vast majority of these individual Jews needed to be saved in order to become part of true Israel (spiritual Israel). Our understanding of Romans 10:13 must come from our understanding of Joel 2:32. Our understanding of these two texts cannot be *contradictory.* Our understanding of these two texts must be *complimentary.* The word "call" from Joel 2:32 is translated from the Hebrew word *qara'* (kaw-raw'). The primary meaning of the word simply is to address someone by their name. The purpose of calling on the Name of Jesus is to be saved from God's eternal condemnation in Hell.

The last of the five verbs defining a faith decision to be "born again" is the word RECEIVE. To "receive" the Lord Jesus Christ is to receive His indwelling presence in the Person of the Holy Spirit. This is explain in detail in chapter ten of this book.

"[11] He came unto his own, and his own received him not. [12] But as many as received him, to them gave he power to become the sons of God, *even* to them that believe on his name: [13] Which were born, not of blood, nor of the will of the flesh, nor of the will of man, but of God" (John 1:11-13).

Questions for Discussion

1. Discuss the importance and significance of the word *understanding* in Matthew 13:1-9 as this relates to ensuring a true conversion of the heart.

2. Discuss what is involved in preparing the heart to receive the *seed.*

3. Discuss what is specifically necessary to understand to ensure biblical *repentance* comes forth from the heart.

4. Discuss the two doctrines that must be understood before a person can *believe/rest* in the Gospel of Jesus Christ.

5. Define the meanings of the verbs *confess*, *call*, and *receive* as they define a *faith decision* to be "born again." Then discuss the *action* that defines each of these verbs in their relationship to the Lord Jesus Christ.

Chapter Two

Biblical Examples of Repentance in Conversion

The first aspect of a genuine conversion experience is to comprehend who we are before God and what we have done that deserves God's condemnation of our souls. There are three parables in Luke chapter fifteen detailing the importance of repentance to God. The parables are taught as a response to the questioning of the "Pharisees and scribes" (Luke 15:2) of why Christ "receiveth sinners." We need only read Matthew chapter twenty-three to find out Christ's evaluation of the scribes and Pharisees as self-righteous hypocrites. Therefore, it is easy to see that the purpose of these three parables in Luke chapter fifteen is to deal with the inability of the self-righteous moralist to see himself as a sinner before God even condemned as the worst of sinners.

> 11 And he said, A certain man had two sons: 12 And the
> younger of them said to *his* father, Father, give me the
> portion of goods that falleth *to me*. And he divided unto them
> *his* living. 13 And not many days after the younger son
> gathered all together, and took his journey into a far country,
> and there wasted his substance with riotous living. 14 And
> when he had spent all, there arose a mighty famine in that
> land; and he began to be in want. 15 And he went and joined
> himself to a citizen of that country; and he sent him into his
> fields to feed swine. 16 And he would fain have filled his
> belly with the husks that the swine did eat: and no man gave
> unto him. 17 And when he came to himself, he said, How
> many hired servants of my father's have bread enough and
> to spare, and I perish with hunger! 18 I will arise and go to
> my father, and will say unto him, Father, I have sinned
> against heaven, and before thee, 19 And am no more worthy
> to be called thy son: make me as one of thy hired servants.
> 20 And he arose, and came to his father. But when he was yet
> a great way off, his father saw him, and had compassion, and
> ran, and fell on his neck, and kissed him. 21 And the son said

unto him, Father, I have sinned against heaven, and in thy sight, and am no more worthy to be called thy son (Luke 15:11-20).

The prodigal son's change of mind resulted in a change of action that corresponded with his new evaluation of himself. He no longer came to the father based upon what he deserved. In repentance, he came to the father solely based on grace and making an appeal to his grace. The father responds in grace. The picture before us is one of genuine salvation.

We are told in Luke 15:17 that the prodigal son "came to himself." This is critically essential in a genuine conversion experience. Often people rescue those in the midst of the consequences of their sins before those people come to see their sins as the cause of their life disasters. Cognizance of sin is the recognition that sin has temporal and eternal consequences connected to these actions. Such cognizance of our sins brings the sinner to make a biblical evaluation of his character that has brought him to the situation in which he now exists. It is not enough to want to merely escape the situation caused by his depravity. Genuine repentance wants to escape the depravity that caused the situation. If we miss this point, we fail to understand genuine repentance. Such a person will soon be back, drinking from that same old corrupting fountain.

Therefore, it is so difficult for the self-righteous *religionists* to come to repentance. The self-righteous *religionist* views himself as a morally good person. Jesus often dealt with this failure in the mindset of the Jews. In Matthew chapter nineteen, Jesus has a conversation with a very rich "young man." The "young man" comes to Jesus and acknowledges Jesus as a "master," or a teaching rabbi, that understands the will of God. His question is found in Matthew 19:16, "what good thing shall I do, that I may have eternal life?" At first, Jesus bypasses his question and addresses the root of his problem. The "young man" addressed Jesus as "Good {*agathos*} Master." Herein lies the first necessity in genuine repentance. Jesus responds to the young man's statement with a remarkable truth. This truth confronted the very heart and soul of the misconceptions of thinking in the self-righteous *religionists* to coming to repentance. Jesus says, "Why callest thou me good? *there is* none good but one, *that is*, God" (Matthew 19:17). Only God is morally good *all the time. All the time* is the singular qualification for being self-righteous. Only God is self-righteous. Everyone else is a sinner because no one else but God is good *all the time*.

Jesus then exemplifies what moral goodness does in Matthew 19:21; "If thou wilt be perfect {*teleios; morally complete*}, go *and* sell that thou hast, and give to the poor, and thou shalt have treasure in heaven: and come *and* follow me." This exemplifies God's moral perfection in God's grace. The "poor" were viewed by the self-righteous Jews as being sinners living in the consequences of their sin. In other words, the Pharisees believed people were poor because they lived in sin, broke the Law, and were under God's chastisement. This was due to a misunderstanding of the "blessing and a curse" promise of God to the *nation* of Israel in the Mosaic Covenant. The Jews applied the "blessing and a curse" promise of God to individuals.

> [26] Behold, I set before you {*plural, refers to all of the nation of Israel*} this day a blessing and a curse; [27] A blessing, if ye obey the commandments of the LORD your God, which I command you this day: [28] And a curse {*removal or withdrawal of blessings*}, if ye will not obey the commandments of the LORD your God, but turn aside out of the way which I command you this day, to go after other gods, which ye have not known. [29] And it shall come to pass, when the LORD thy God hath brought thee in unto the land whither thou goest to possess it, that thou shalt put the blessing upon mount Gerizim, and the curse upon mount Ebal. [30] *Are* they not on the other side Jordan, by the way where the sun goeth down, in the land of the Canaanites, which dwell in the champaign {*the sterile valley of Jordan*} over against Gilgal, beside the plains of Moreh? [31] For ye shall pass over Jordan to go in to possess the land which the LORD your God giveth you, and ye shall possess it, and dwell therein. [32] And ye shall observe to do all the statutes and judgments which I set before you this day (Deuteronomy 11:26-32).

Therefore, when Jesus told the young man to sacrifice all of his earthly treasures to acquire the heavenly treasure of eternal life, the young man started to *choke to death* on his self-righteousness. Christ Jesus was telling him that a change of mind about his wealth would result in using that wealth to exemplify God's loving grace to the undeserving sinner. This required more than just a change of thinking, but rather a change of mind that was accompanied by giving his wealth to benefit the poor. Of course, doing so would bring him into poverty and total dependence upon God for his own sustenance. This would require that he see himself in the degradation of his own spiritual poverty before God even in his temporal wealth. This is why Jesus said to the disciples in the next few verses of Matthew 19:23 and 24, "Verily I say unto you, That a rich man shall hardly {*duskolos; with great or extreme difficulty*} enter into the kingdom of heaven. And again I say unto you, It is easier for a camel to go through the eye of a needle, than for a rich man to enter into the kingdom of God {*get saved*}."

Jesus was exemplifying how this false notion of self-righteousness, and the false interpretation of wealth as a blessing upon self-righteousness, would keep the Moralist from seeing his true sinfulness before God and repent of the sin of self-righteousness. The first point of genuine repentance is to understand "*there is* none good but one, *that is*, God" (Matthew 19:17).

Certainly, we can see this repentance in the life of the Apostle Paul. Paul reflects a completely different opinion of himself after he is "born again." Paul calls himself the chief "sinner" in I Timothy 1:15. Paul stated his previous perverted opinion of himself and his false understanding of the Law in Philippians 3:4-6.

> [4] Though I might also have <u>confidence in the flesh</u>. If any other man thinketh that he hath whereof he might trust in the flesh, I more: [5] Circumcised the eighth day, of the stock of Israel, *of* the tribe of Benjamin, an Hebrew of the Hebrews; as touching the law, a Pharisee; [6] Concerning zeal, persecuting the church; touching the righteousness which is in the law, blameless (Philippians 3:4-6).

Paul's statement in Philippians 3:4-8 reflects the dark blindness of self-righteousness - just how far short even these (man-kind righteousness) come from the glory of God (Romans 3:23; God-kind righteousness). After salvation, Paul makes a statement regarding all truly repentant believers in their evaluation of themselves before God; "For we are the {*true spiritual*} circumcision, which worship God in the spirit, and rejoice in Christ Jesus, and have no confidence in the flesh" (Philippians 3:3). Self-righteousness is incapable of sanctifying anyone before God. Self-righteousness will bring nothing but God's loathing condemnation. Paul understood this because this was the substance of his very first conversation with the resurrected and glorified Lord Jesus on the Damascus road when he got saved. Paul rehearsed his conversion as he spoke to King Agrippa in Acts chapter twenty-six. After which Paul was committed to the same message and the same repentance that brought about his own conversion.

> 12 Whereupon as I went to Damascus with authority and commission from the chief priests, 13 At midday, O king, I saw in the way a light from heaven, above the brightness of the sun, shining round about me and them which journeyed with me. 14 And when we were all fallen to the earth, I heard a voice speaking unto me, and saying in the Hebrew tongue, Saul, Saul, why persecutest thou me? *it is* hard for thee to kick against the pricks. 15 And I said, Who art thou, Lord? And he said, I am Jesus whom thou persecutest. 16 But rise, and stand upon thy feet: for I have appeared unto thee for this purpose, to make thee a minister and a witness both of these things which thou hast seen, and of those things in the which I will appear unto thee; 17 Delivering thee from the people, and *from* the Gentiles, unto whom now I send thee, 18 To open their eyes, *and* to turn *them* from darkness to light, and *from* the power of Satan unto God, that they may {*condition upon their turning; not just a change of mind*} receive forgiveness of sins, and inheritance among them which are sanctified by faith that is in me. 19 Whereupon, O king Agrippa, I was not disobedient unto the heavenly vision: 20 But shewed first unto them of Damascus, and at Jerusalem, and throughout all the coasts of Judaea, and *then*

to the Gentiles, that they should repent and turn to God, **and** do works meet for {*comparable to; or living which aligns with their*} repentance (Acts 26:12-20).

Certainly, the text reveals that genuine repentance is always expected to reflect a genuine *change of life*, not just a *change of mind.* Genuine repentance involves turning "from darkness to light and from the power of Satan unto God" (Acts 26:18), not just a change of mind. Action is involved in genuine repentance. In other words, a change in direction is the outcome of genuine repentance.

We also know that this repentance text is not referring to merely turning away from trust in the "works of the Law" (Moralism and ritualism Sacerdotalism) because the text is referring to the Gentiles (Acts 26:20). The Gentiles were not trusting in the "works of the Law" for their standing before God. The Gentiles needed to repent of idolatry and the licentious - fornicating lifestyles that accompanied idolatry.

The word fornication often simply meant the *practices of idolatry*. The Greek word translated "fornication" in the New Testament books is the word *porneia* (por-ni'-ah). The word often simply means to practice the licentious, lustful sexual perversions of idolatry. Turning completely away from this lifestyle and its practices was included in genuine repentance. These practices had become common in Israel prior to the Babylonian captivity. God's chastisement of the nation of Israel in the Babylonian captivity was intended to bring them to repentance and return them to pure worship of Jehovah and obedience to Him. This is the biblical context of repentance of sin. Repentance is a turning "from darkness to light, and *from* the power of Satan unto God" (Acts 26:18). The Greek word translated "turn" in Acts 26:18 is *epistrepho* (ep-ee-stref'-o). This same Greek word is often translated "converted" as it is in Acts 3:19.

In Acts 3:19, the subject of repentance to conversion is about the Person and redemptive work Jesus Christ in His death, burial, and resurrection/glorification. This text addresses the Jews and their rejection of the Person and work of their promised Messiah.

12 And when Peter saw *it* {*the wonder at the healing of the*
man lame from birth}, he answered unto the people, Ye men
of Israel, why marvel ye at this? or why look ye so earnestly
on us, as though by our own power or holiness we had made
this man to walk? 13 The God of Abraham, and of Isaac, and
of Jacob, the God of our fathers, hath glorified his Son Jesus;
whom ye delivered up, and denied him in the presence of
Pilate, when he was determined to let *him* go. 14 But ye
{*plural*} denied the Holy One and the Just, and desired a
murderer to be granted unto you; 15 And killed the Prince of
life, whom God hath raised from the dead; whereof we are
witnesses. 16 And **his name through faith in his name hath**
made this man strong, whom ye see and know: yea, **the**
faith which is by him hath given him this perfect
soundness in the presence of you all. 17 And now, brethren,
I wot that through ignorance ye did *it*, as *did* also your rulers.
18 But those things, which God before had shewed by the
mouth of all his prophets, that Christ should suffer, he hath
so fulfilled. 19 Repent {*metanoeo*} ye therefore, and be
converted {*epistrepho*}, **that** your sins may be blotted out,
when the times of refreshing {*recovery of breath*; *the*
implication is spiritually revived from death} shall come
from the presence of the Lord; 20 And he shall send Jesus
Christ {*the second coming*}, which before was preached
unto you: 21 Whom the heaven must receive until the times
of restitution {*the spiritual reconstruction of national Israel*
and the restoration of dominion to humanity through the last
Adam, which is Christ Jesus} of all things, which God hath
spoken by the mouth of all his holy prophets since the world
began {*Genesis 3:15*}. 22 For Moses truly said unto the
fathers {*Deuteronomy 18:18*}, A prophet shall the Lord your
God raise up unto you of your brethren, like unto me; him
shall ye hear in all things whatsoever he shall say unto you.
23 And it shall come to pass, *that* every soul, which will not
hear that prophet, shall be destroyed from among the people.
24 Yea, and all the prophets from Samuel and those that
follow after, as many as have spoken, have likewise foretold
of these days. 25 Ye are the children of the prophets, and of
the covenant which God made with our fathers, saying unto

> Abraham, And in thy seed shall all the kindreds of the earth be blessed. [26] Unto you first God, having raised up his Son Jesus, sent him to bless you, in turning away {*apostrepho; to turn away or turn around*} every one of you **from** his iniquities (Acts 3:12-26).

Again, the pattern in Scripture is that biblical repentance always results in turning away from sin. Biblical repentance is not merely a *change of mind*, but also a *change of direction.* If a person's life has no *change of direction*, repentance is not genuine and conversion has not taken place.

Questions for Discussion

1. Discuss the parable of what is commonly called the Parable of the Prodigal Son and why the subject of the parable is really on the other son defining the substance of repentance of self-righteousness.

2. Discuss how the fact revealed in Luke 15:17 that the prodigal son "came to himself" manifests genuine repentance of sin.

3. In the parable of the *Two Sons* of Luke 15:11-20, which of the two sons presents the most difficult problem for humility and genuine repentance? Discuss why.

4. Discuss Matthew 19:21 and of what this rich young ruler needed to repent.

5. Discuss how Acts 26:12-20 reveals that genuine repentance is always expected to reflect a genuine *change of life*, not just a *change of mind.*

Chapter Three

Understanding Corruption and Repentance

Leading a person to ultimately call upon the Name of the Lord for the gift of salvation must be preceded by several other very important and essential decisions. These decisions must be born out of clear understanding of God's view of humanity as sinners condemned to eternal separation from Him in a place referred to in God's Word as Hell. Hell was created for fallen angels and their leader. Angels are spiritual beings. Fallen angels are spiritual beings who corrupted themselves by refusing God's *chain of command* in giving Adam dominion over God's creation.

To corrupt God's created order of dominion, Satan deceived Eve who took leadership of her husband and led Adam into sin by direct disobedience to God's command. Adam's *nature was corrupted.* Adam became a *sinner by nature.* In other words, from that point forward in time Adam and all that came from his loins were sinners by nature and corrupt by nature (Romans 5:12). Adam and all his descendants became CORPOREAL.

The word *corporeal* simply means having, consisting of, or relating to a physical material body: not spiritual, not immaterial or intangible. Although humanity still retains a spiritual aspect of existence, humanity's spirituality was corrupted. The human body was cursed to die. The human emotions became selfish. Human desires were corrupted through the "lust the flesh, and the lust of the eyes, and the pride of life" (I John 2:16). The whole of the original creation was cursed of God to ultimately be "dissolved" and "melt with fervent heat" (II Peter 3:10-12). It is into this scenario of human corruption that God's grace and mercy is revealed to humanity through His promise of redemption offered as a gift "through faith" (Ephesians 2:8). Essential to understanding the faith decision is understanding how repentance fits into redemption from this corruption and the consequences of that corruption.

> [9] **The Lord is not slack concerning his promise, as some men count slackness; but is longsuffering to us-ward, not**

willing that any should perish, but that all should come to repentance. [10] But the day of the Lord will come as a thief in the night; in the which the heavens shall pass away with a great noise, and the elements shall melt with fervent heat, the earth also and the works that are therein shall be burned up. [11] *Seeing* then *that* all these things shall be dissolved, what manner *of persons* ought ye to be in *all* holy conversation and godliness, [12] Looking for and hasting unto the coming of the day of God, wherein the heavens being on fire shall be dissolved, and the elements shall melt with fervent heat? [13] Nevertheless we, according to his promise, look for new heavens and a new earth, wherein dwelleth righteousness (II Peter 3:9-13).

Genuine, *God-produced* repentance that affects the heart is the outcome of understanding the nature of the corruption of sin and the complete condemnation of the sinner under the all-encompassing curse of God upon sin. To understand the corruption of humanity through sin is to understand every sinner is guilty before God of a capital offense worthy of eternal separation from God (death). Therefore, repentance involves a change of mind and heart regarding our own ability to change the consequences of condemnation in the curse of God.

[19] Now we know that what things soever the law saith, it saith to them who are under the law {*to somehow achieve God-kind righteousness*}: that every mouth may be stopped {*regarding any claim to having achieved God-kind righteousness*}, and all the world may become guilty before God. [20] Therefore by the deeds of the law there shall no flesh be justified in his sight: for by the law *is* the knowledge of sin. [21] But now the righteousness of God {*God-kind righteousness*} without {*apart from*} the law is manifested, being {*having been*} witnessed by the law and the prophets; [22] Even the righteousness of God *which is* by faith of Jesus Christ unto all and upon all them that believe {*as a gift*}: for there is no difference: [23] **For all have sinned, and come short of the glory of God**; [24] Being justified {*gifted God-kind righteousness*} freely by his grace through the

redemption that is in Christ Jesus: [25] Whom God hath set forth *to be* a propitiation through faith in his blood, to declare his righteousness for the remission of sins that are past, through the forbearance of God; [26] To declare, *I say*, at this time his righteousness: that he might be just, and the justifier of him which believeth in Jesus. [27] Where *is* boasting then? It is excluded. By what law? of works? Nay: but by the law of faith. [28] Therefore we conclude that a man is justified by faith without the deeds of the law (Romans 3:19-28).

Preparing the heart to receive the "seed" through genuine biblical repentance is perhaps the greatest essential to a genuine conversion experience. Without repentance of sin, worldliness, and "dead works," the sinner will never fully understand the Gospel because he will never understand the *good news* that liberates him from the bondage to his own corrupt and fallen nature. Therefore, the Apostle Paul uses almost three full chapters of his Epistle to the Romans to explain the doctrine of condemnation BEFORE he begins to explain the doctrine of salvation. This is preparing the "soil" of the heart for conversion. The sinner must understand the holiness of God and the sinfulness of sin. *Preparing the heart* is picking up the rocks that hardened a person to their sin and harden a person to the work of the Holy Spirit. Preparing the heart is clearing away the thorns and thistles of worldly ambitions that will grow and choke away any possibility for new life to generate to fruition in the heart.

Preparing the heart to receive the "seed" is what biblical repentance is all about. Many have come to think that repentance is merely an intellectual change of the mind about sin, worldliness, and false doctrine. Genuine repentance affects the **mind** (how we think about sin, worldliness, and false doctrine), the **emotions** (how we feel about sin, worldliness, and false doctrine), and **practice** (how we live what we know or believe).

Changing practice is the <u>outcome</u> of genuine repentance and is progressive towards godliness <u>AFTER CONVERSION</u> due to numerous volitional choices. In other words, the way we live our lives **<u>should</u>** progressively be changed by varying degrees as we *grow* to know the Word of God and the God of the Word. However, **until** there is a change of mind that *agrees* with the revealed will of God AND a change of heart that *feels* about sin, worldliness, and false doctrine the way God feels about sin, worldliness, and false doctrine, **repentance is not happening**.

There are varying degrees of this failure revealed in the parable of the Seed and the Soils. **The central focus of the parable is that improperly prepared minds and improperly prepared hearts will result in false conversions due to failure to understand what the Gospel of Jesus Christ accomplishes on the sinner's behalf. False conversions are equally probable without preparation of the sinner's heart through biblical repentance.** Just rushing sinners through the *Romans Road* to get them to *pray the prayer* is a gross injustice against God's redemption.

Parables are simple examples and are not always perfect examples. Parables seek to explain very deep spiritual truths by using common physical examples. These physical illustrations can never fully convey the full depth of the spiritual truth they seek to explain.

> [18] Hear ye therefore the parable of the sower. [19] When any one heareth the word of the kingdom, and **understandeth *it* not**, then cometh the wicked *one*, and catcheth away that which was sown in his heart. This is he which received seed by the way side. [20] But he that received the seed into stony places, the same is he that heareth the word, and anon with joy receiveth it; [21] Yet hath he not root in himself {*no depth of understanding*}, but dureth for a while: for when tribulation or persecution ariseth because of the word, by and by he is offended. [22] He also that received seed among the thorns is he that heareth the word; and the care of this world, and the deceitfulness of riches, choke the word, and he becometh unfruitful. [23] But he that received seed into the good ground is he that heareth the word, and **understandeth *it***; which also beareth fruit, and bringeth forth, some an hundredfold, some sixty, some thirty (Matthew 13:18-23).

In other words, inward transformation/regeneration can never take place without this *understanding*. **The critical detail**

here is that *understanding* with the head must become *understanding* with the heart before saving faith is produced through the operations of the Holy Spirit of God (i.e., germination of the Seed or regeneration). The proper response to the Gospel is what defines *believing*, or what is more commonly referred to as *saving faith*.

The first verb in a faith decision to be "born again" is the verb REPENT. There MUST be repentance of sin (Romans 1:18-32). There MUST be repentance of one's trust in his own Moralism (Romans 2:1-29). There MUST be repentance of one's trust in sacramental rituals as means of conferring the grace of God in salvation (Romans 3:1-20). Perhaps the simplest way to explain repentance is that genuine repentance is *birthed* out of the knowledge of two basic Bible truths. If we want true Bible repentance produced in our lives, we must understand these two basic Bible truths and pursue that understanding from the revelation of God's Word.

> **1.** We must understand how vile and disgusting our sinfulness is in the eyes of God.
> **2.** We must understand the holiness and sanctity of God.

> [10] As it is written, There is **none** righteous, no, **not one**: [11]
> There is **none** that understandeth, there is **none** that seeketh
> after God. [12] They are **all** gone out of the way, they are
> **together** become unprofitable; there is **none** that doeth
> good, no, **not one.** [13] Their throat *is* an open sepulchre; with
> their tongues they have used deceit; the poison of asps *is*
> under their lips: [14] Whose mouth *is* full of cursing and
> bitterness: [15] Their feet *are* swift to shed blood: [16]
> Destruction and misery *are* in their ways: [17] And the way of
> peace have they not known: [18] There is no fear of God before
> their eyes (Romans 3:10-18).

Until people see themselves the way God sees them, they will never repent the way God expects them to repent! Genuine repentance sees ourselves just as God sees us. There are no meritorious qualities about us that make us lovely to God or even loveable. We are horrible, wicked, vile, puss-buckets of putridity.

God does not love us because we are loveable. God loves us because He is love. Yet, God sees **what we can be** if we grasp genuine repentance, get "born again," and begin to live by His enabling grace.

The Greek word *epistrepho* (ep-ee-stref'-o), translated "converted" in Matthew 13:15, literally means *to be turned around.* This conversion cannot happen apart from genuine repentance. Repentance is the beginning point of that *turning around.* Peter made this distinction in Acts 3:19; "Repent ye therefore, and be converted, that your sins may be blotted out . . ." Each of the other four verbs in a faith decision also reflect a turning around in what we think and believe.

Repentance is essential to correct two false beliefs. First, everyone is a sinner by act and by nature. Therefore, no one can ever be as righteous as God requires because we all begin as sinners. David said, "Behold, I was shapen in iniquity; and in sin did my mother conceive me" (Psalm 51:5). David was not only a sinner by action (Psalm 51:1-4), but sin was an integral part of his fallen nature even at the point of his conception in his mother's womb.

> The wicked are estranged {*turned aside, profane*} from the womb: they go astray {*their inward depravity causes them to go astray*} as soon as they be born, speaking lies (Psalm 58:3).

Second, everyone must turn away (repent) from false beliefs about salvific religious rituals (Ritualism or Sacramentalism). Everyone must also repent of being able to achieve the kind of lifestyle that might somehow cause God to see such a person favorably and allow them into heaven. This is what God condemns when He speaks against legalism or externalism in the Bible in using of the words "dead works."

> [10] Called of God an high priest after the order of Melchisedec. [11] Of whom we have many things to say, and hard to be uttered, seeing ye are dull of hearing. [12] For when for the time ye ought to be teachers, ye have need that one teach you again which *be* the first principles of the oracles

of God; and are become such as have need of milk, and not
of strong meat. [13] For every one that useth milk *is* unskilful
in the word of righteousness: for he is a babe. [14] But strong
meat belongeth to them that are of full age, *even* those who
by reason of use have their senses exercised to discern both
good and evil. [1] Therefore leaving the principles of the
doctrine of Christ, let us go on unto perfection; not laying
again the foundation of repentance from dead works, and of
faith toward God, [2] Of the doctrine of baptisms, and of laying
on of hands, and of resurrection of the dead, and of eternal
judgment. [3] And this will we do, if God permit (Hebrews
5:10-6:3).

The context of the Epistle to the Hebrews is historically about A.D. 64. The doctrinal context addresses the early corruption of Jewish Christians by Judaizers that had convinced many Jewish Christians that the Mosaic Covenant was still part of Christianity. Therefore, Jewish believers still had to keep the ritual aspects of the Law in offering animal sacrifices, circumcising, keeping the Holy Days, and being faithful to the Jewish Temple Order and Synagogues. The Jewish Temple Order had corrupted the Mosaic Covenant by making these Old Covenant practices necessary to salvation. Salvation became a process rather than a gift received by faith. Paul addresses this in his Epistle to the Galatians and absolutely condemns this false doctrine. In Paul's Epistle to the Hebrews, he equates a return to the Mosaic Covenant and its practices to a false profession of faith in the finished work of Christ.

[11] But when Peter was come to Antioch, I withstood him to
the face, because he was to be blamed. [12] For before that
certain came from James, he did eat with the Gentiles: but
when they were come, he withdrew and separated himself,
fearing them which were of the circumcision. [13] And the
other Jews dissembled likewise with him; insomuch that
Barnabas also was carried away with their dissimulation. [14]
But when I saw that they walked not uprightly according to
the truth of the gospel, I said unto Peter before *them* all, If
thou, being a Jew, livest after the manner of Gentiles, and

not as do the Jews, why compellest thou the Gentiles to live as do the Jews? [15] We *who are* Jews by nature, and not sinners of the Gentiles, [16] Knowing that a man is not justified by the works of the law, but by the faith of Jesus Christ, even we have believed in Jesus Christ, **that we might be justified by the faith of Christ, and not by the works of the law: for by the works of the law shall no flesh be justified** (Galatians 2:11-16).

The intent of the Epistle to the Galatians is to confront the corruption of the Law by exposing the corrupted priesthood of Israel who taught that Law keeping (doing the *works* of the Law) would result in salvation. Nothing could be further from the truth. The Mosaic Covenant was added to the Abrahamic Covenant because of repetitive transgressions (Galatians 3:19) due to ignorance of what was sin.

[1] O foolish Galatians, who hath bewitched you, that ye should not obey the truth, before whose eyes Jesus Christ hath been evidently set forth, crucified among you? [2] This only would I learn of you, **Received ye the Spirit by the works of the law, or by the hearing of faith**? [3] Are ye so foolish? having begun in the Spirit, are ye now made perfect by the flesh? [4] Have ye suffered so many things in vain? if *it be* yet in vain. [5] He therefore that ministereth to you the Spirit, and worketh miracles among you, *doeth he it* by the works of the law, or by the hearing of faith? [6] **Even as Abraham believed God, and it was accounted to him for righteousness.** [7] Know ye therefore that they which are of faith, the same are the children of Abraham. [8] And the scripture, foreseeing that God would justify the heathen through faith, preached before the gospel unto Abraham, *saying*, In thee shall all nations be blessed. [9] So then they which be of faith are blessed with faithful Abraham. [10] **For as many as are of the works of the law are under the curse: for it is written, Cursed *is* every one that continueth** {*stay in the same place*} **not in all things which are written in the book of the law to do them.** [11] **But that no man is justified by the law in the sight of God, *it is***

evident: for, The just shall live by faith. [12] And the law is not of faith: but, The man that doeth them shall live in them. [13] Christ hath redeemed us from the curse of the law, being made a curse for us: for it is written, Cursed *is* every one that hangeth on a tree: [14] That the blessing of Abraham might come on the Gentiles through Jesus Christ; that we might receive the promise of the Spirit through faith (Galatians 3:1-14).

[1] Stand fast therefore in the liberty wherewith Christ hath made us free, and be not entangled again with the yoke of bondage. [2] Behold, I Paul say unto you, that **if ye be circumcised, Christ shall profit you nothing**. [3] For I testify again to every man that is circumcised, that he is a debtor to do the whole law. [4] Christ is become of no effect unto you, whosoever of you are justified by the law; ye are fallen from grace. [5] For we through the Spirit wait for the hope of righteousness by faith. [6] For in Jesus Christ neither circumcision availeth any thing, nor uncircumcision; but faith which worketh by love. [7] Ye did run well; who did hinder you that ye should not obey the truth? [8] This persuasion *cometh* not of him that calleth you. [9] A little leaven leaveneth the whole lump (Galatians 5:1-9).

The person who has repented of the "dead works" of Moralism and Ritualism has abandoned all trust in their own personal righteous acts for salvation. Such a repentant person understands that he has been deceived along with thousands of others. Such repentance should result in loathing the false teaching that deceives. Such repentance should result in the willingness to confront those teaching the deception just as does the Apostle Paul in both the Epistle to the Hebrews and the Epistle to the Galatians. The person who has repented of the "dead works" of Moralism and Ritualism has abandoned all trust in any religious ritual or sacrament to aid them in their salvation or as the means of being regenerated. Repentance understands that these types of beliefs do not bring a person closer to salvation. Instead these types of beliefs just make it more difficult for someone to get saved by grace through faith. Therefore, genuine repentance would not allow a repentant person to remain in local churches teaching such deception that hinders people from trusting solely in the finished work of Christ.

> [13] But woe unto you, scribes and Pharisees, hypocrites! for ye shut up the kingdom of heaven against men: **for ye neither go in *yourselves*, neither suffer ye them that are entering to go in**. [14] Woe unto you, scribes and Pharisees, hypocrites! for ye devour widows' houses, and for a pretence make long prayer: therefore **ye shall receive the greater damnation**. [15] Woe unto you, scribes and Pharisees, hypocrites! for ye compass sea and land to make one proselyte, and **when he is made, ye make him twofold more the child of hell than yourselves** (Matthew 23:13-15).

It is certainly true that the clear majority of Bible texts referring to the necessity of repentance preceding salvation demand repentance of trust in "dead works" (Ritualism and Moralism as aides to justification before God). Justification is the gift of *God-kind righteousness* to the repentant believer. Justification in the gift of *God-kind righteousness* can only be **received**. It can never be **achieved**.

The message of Law/works repentance is addressed to those who had been corrupted by the false teaching that justification could be *achieved*. This corruption of the Law was true primarily of the Jewish Pharisees. It applies to modern professions within Christianity of those trusting in some religious *sacrament* to confer God's grace to the professing believer. In such cases, this corruption almost always sees salvation as a *process* rather than an *event*.

However, there are clearly Bible texts where sinful acts are subject of repentance. Repentance of these sinful acts must precede salvation. This is revealed in Paul's testimony of salvation to king Agrippa in Acts chapter twenty-six. In this chapter, Paul gives the details of his commissioning by Christ to go to the Gentiles. The Gentiles did not believe in salvation by "the works of the Law" as did the Jews.

12 Whereupon as I went to Damascus with authority and
commission from the chief priests, 13 At midday, O king, I
saw in the way a light from heaven, above the brightness of
the sun, shining round about me and them which journeyed
with me. 14 And when we were all fallen to the earth, I heard
a voice {*Jesus*} speaking unto me, and saying in the Hebrew
tongue, Saul, Saul, why persecutest thou me? *it is* hard for
thee to kick against the pricks. 15 And I said, Who art thou,
Lord? And he said, I am Jesus whom thou persecutest. 16 But
rise, and stand upon thy feet: for **I have appeared unto thee
for this purpose**, to make thee a minister and a witness both
of these things which thou hast seen, and of those things in
the which I will appear unto thee; 17 Delivering thee from the
people, and *from* the Gentiles, **unto whom now I send thee**,
18 To open their eyes, *and* **to turn *them* from darkness to
light**, and ***from* the power of Satan unto God**, that they may
receive forgiveness of sins, and inheritance among them
which are sanctified by faith that is in me. 19 Whereupon, O
king Agrippa, I was not disobedient unto the heavenly
vision: 20 But shewed first unto them of Damascus, and at
Jerusalem, and throughout all the coasts of Judaea, and *then*
to the Gentiles, **that they should repent and turn to God,
and do works meet for repentance**. 21 For these causes the
Jews caught me in the temple, and went about to kill *me*. 22
Having therefore obtained help of God, I continue unto this
day, witnessing both to small and great, saying none other
things than those which the prophets and Moses did say
should come: 23 That Christ should suffer, *and* that he should
be the first that should rise from the dead, and should **shew
light unto the people, and to the Gentiles** (Acts 26:12-23).

The key verse in the text is Acts 26:18 where Paul say his commission from Christ was to "turn *them* from darkness to light." This is clearly speaking of the spiritual ignorance of the righteousness of God that accompanies idolatry and paganism. These false beliefs allowed the Gentiles to participate in all types of licentious practices. It is all these licentious practices from which the Gentiles needed to *turn* (repent). The word "turn" is from the Greek word *epistrepho* (ep-ee-stref'-o) meaning to *turn about* or *be converted.* This all equally applies to Paul's sermon on Mar's hill in Acts 17:22-31.

> 22 Then Paul stood in the midst of Mars' hill, and said, *Ye* men of Athens, I perceive that in all things ye are too superstitious. 23 For as I passed by, and beheld your devotions, I found an altar with this inscription, TO THE UNKNOWN GOD. **Whom therefore ye ignorantly worship, him declare I unto you**. 24 God that made the world and all things therein, seeing that he is Lord of heaven and earth, dwelleth not in temples made with hands; 25 Neither is worshipped with men's hands, as though he needed any thing, seeing he giveth to all life, and breath, and all things; 26 **And hath made of one blood all nations of men for to dwell on all the face of the earth**, and hath determined the times before appointed, and the bounds of their habitation; 27 That they should seek the Lord, if haply they might feel after him, and find him, though he be not far from every one of us: 28 For in him we live, and move, and have our being; as certain also of your own poets have said, For we are also his offspring. 29 Forasmuch then as we are the offspring of God, we ought not to think that the Godhead is like unto gold, or silver, or stone, graven by art and man's device. 30 **And the times of this ignorance God winked at; but now commandeth all men every where to repent**: 31 Because he hath appointed a day, in the which he will judge the world in righteousness by *that* man {Jesus} whom he hath ordained; *whereof* he hath given assurance unto all *men*, in that he hath raised him from the dead (Acts 17:22-31).

Questions for Discussion

1. Discuss the meaning of the word *corporeal* as it relates to the corruption of human spirituality and why understanding this is important to understanding biblical repentance.

2. Discuss the differences between *God-produced* repentance that affects the heart and mere remorse for sin.

3. Discuss the differences between repentance of sin, worldliness, and "dead works," and why understanding these differences are essential for the sinner to fully understand the Gospel.

4. Explain the difference between understanding repentance *with the head* and understanding repentance *from the heart.*

5. Discuss why repentance of "the works of the law" is essential to faith in the Gospel of Jesus Christ and why those that continue to trust in their own Moralism, or some religious ritual or sacrament to be saved, manifest unbelief not faith.

Chapter Four

Believing with the Heart

The second verb involved in a faith decision is the verb BELIEVE. Is this merely believing in the death, burial, and resurrection of Jesus, or is this believing in what the death, burial, and resurrection of Jesus accomplishes? It is foolish to expect people to be able to grasp the theological meaning of believing in the death, burial, and resurrection of Jesus without an explanation. To believe in the death, burial, and resurrection of Jesus is more than merely believing in the historical reality of these historical facts. There are a few objective facts connected to the death, burial, and resurrection of Jesus that must be known and understood before a person can believe in those objective facts.

1. The vicarious nature of the death, burial, and resurrection of Jesus
2. The propitiation of God's wrath through the death, burial, and resurrection of Jesus
3. The gift of justification through faith in the death, burial, and resurrection of Jesus

The word *believe* reflects and implies a *turning away* from false beliefs regarding religious "works" (Moralism and Ritualism). The word *believe* reflects and implies a *turning to* believe **solely** in what Christ Jesus accomplished in His death, burial, and resurrection. This *turning away* from "works" is crucial to defining the meaning and practical intent of the word "believe." Therefore, to believe in a truth it is necessary to reject everything contrary to that truth. Since things that are different are not the same, two contradicting statements cannot both be true.

The vicarious nature of the death, burial, and resurrection of Jesus is the fulfillment of the Old Testament types in the sinless and perfect substitute Lamb offered in sacrifice for the sins of the people. The word vicarious simply means *to suffer in place of another; taking the place of another person or thing; acting or serving as a substitute*. The nature of the vicarious sacrifice of

Christ is also revealed in numerous Bible texts that can be used to show that Jesus died *in the place of the sinner*. Every person wanting to learn how to lead people to saving faith in Christ should learn and memorize these verses on the vicarious nature of the death, burial, and resurrection of Jesus Christ. At the least, the soul winner should be familiar with these texts and find these passages in their Bibles to read them. A good practice would be to remember Romans 5:6-8 and make marginal notes near that text to remind you of the other references.

> [6] For when we were yet without strength, in due time Christ died **for the ungodly**. [7] For scarcely for a righteous man will one die: yet peradventure for a good man some would even dare to die. [8] But God commendeth his love toward us, in that, **while we were yet sinners**, **Christ died for us** (Romans 5:6-8).

> [13] Christ hath redeemed us from the curse of the law, **being made a curse for us**: for it is written, Cursed *is* every one that hangeth on a tree: [14] That the blessing of Abraham might come on the Gentiles through Jesus Christ; that we might receive the promise of the Spirit through faith (Galatians 3:13-14).

> [21] For even hereunto were ye called: because Christ also **suffered for us**, leaving us an example, that ye should follow his steps: [22] Who did no sin, neither was guile found in his mouth: [23] Who, when he was reviled, reviled not again; when he suffered, he threatened not; but committed *himself* to him that judgeth righteously: [24] Who his **own self bare our sins in his own body on the tree**, that we, being dead to sins, should live unto righteousness: **by whose stripes ye were healed** (I Peter 2:21-24).

One of the great unfathomable truths of redemption is how Jesus could pay the "wages of death" substitutionally for all sinners. How this is accomplished within the realm of God's sovereign justice is nowhere explained in Scripture. We are simply told that Jesus, the incarnate Son of God, accomplished this wonder of God's grace, to our amazement, and we are to believe this incredible truth and rest in its reality.

> For Christ also hath **once suffered for sins, the just for the unjust**, that he might bring us to God, being put to death in the flesh, but quickened by the Spirit (I Peter 3:18).

The great importance of I Peter 3:18 in the revelation of redemptive truths is that the Jesus "once suffered for sins." Therefore, the work of redemption is now a "finished" (John 19:30) work needing nothing more. Jesus' substitutionary death for sinners is a *perfect sacrifice* in that this *one sacrifice* has "by one offering he {*Jesus*} hath perfected {*perfect tense*} for ever them that are sanctified" (Hebrews 10:14). The Old Testament typical animal sacrifices could never remove the penalty of sin just as Scripture proclaims. "For *it is* not possible that the blood of bulls and of goats should take away sins" (Hebrews 10:4).

> [4] Surely **he hath borne** {*prophetic perfect*} **our griefs**, and **carried our sorrows**: yet we did esteem him stricken {*the idea is that they thought Jesus was dying for His own sins, when He was in fact dying for ours; vs. 5-6*}, smitten of God, and afflicted. [5] But he *was* **wounded for our transgressions**, *he was* **bruised for our iniquities**: the **chastisement of our peace *was* upon him**; and **with his stripes we are healed**. [6] All we like sheep have gone astray; we have turned every one to his own way; and **the LORD hath laid on him the iniquity of us all** (Isaiah 53:4-6).

To believe the Gospel is also to believe **with UNDERSTANDING** what the Gospel accomplishes *God-ward* in **propitiation** and *man-ward* in **justification**. To present the Gospel is to present what the Gospel accomplishes first in satisfying God's wrath upon sin (propitiation) and the impartation of God-kind righteousness to the believing sinner in the indwelling Spirit of God (justification).

The word *propitiation* is an important word necessary to understanding and believing the Gospel of Jesus Christ. The English word propitiation is only found three times in the King

James Bible. The English word propitiation is translated from the Greek word *hilasterion* (hil-as-tay'-ree-on). This word is best identified as "the place of propitiation." The theological meaning of the word is *the satisfaction of the just judgment of death from the Law for sins against God* (Romans 3:23 and 6:23). The *place* of propitiation is the Body of Jesus on the Cross of Calvary. This is made clear by Romans 3:21-26.

> 21 But now {*in the incarnation, death, burial, and resurrection of Jesus*} the righteousness of God without {*apart from*} the law is manifested {*made apparent in the incarnation, death, burial, and resurrection of Jesus}*, being witnessed by the law and the prophets; 22 Even the righteousness of God *which is* by faith of Jesus Christ unto all and upon all them that believe: for there is no difference {*Jew or Gentile*}: 23 For all have sinned, and come short of the glory of God; 24 Being justified freely by his grace through the redemption that is in Christ Jesus: 25 Whom God hath set forth {*on the Cross*} *to be* a {*the place of*} propitiation through faith in his blood, to declare his righteousness for the remission {*passing over*} of sins that are past {*before the incarnation, death, burial, and resurrection of Jesus*}, through the forbearance {*God endured the sin without executing its judgment*} of God; 26 To declare, *I say*, at this time his righteousness: that he might be just, and the justifier of him which believeth in Jesus (Romans 3:21-26).

The *means* of propitiation is the substitutionary death and the application of the shed Blood of Jesus to the literal Judgment Seat of God in Heaven (Hebrews 9:12) turning that Judgment Seat into the Mercy Seat of God's grace. It is through this means that God can justly offer the gift of justification to the believing sinner in the impartation of God-kind righteousness through the indwelling of the Holy Spirit. The means of this propitiation is revealed in I John 2:2 and 4:10. In both these texts, the Greek word translated "propitiation" is *hilasmos* (hil-as-mos'). In both cases, the word refers to Jesus in His death, burial, and resurrection as *that which propitiates God.* The point is that God's judgment of eternal condemnation and wrath upon sin is perfectly and righteously satisfied in the substitutionary death of Jesus. Jesus became both our Judgment Seat and our Mercy Seat through faith in His Blood.

> [1] My little children, these things write I unto you, that ye sin not. And if any man sin, we have an advocate with the Father, Jesus Christ the righteous: [2] And he is the propitiation {*that which propitiates God*} for our sins: and not for ours only, but also for *the sins of* the whole world (I John 2:1-3).

> Herein is love, not that we loved God, but that he loved us, and sent his Son *to be* the propitiation {*that which propitiates God*} for our sins (I John 4:10).

The word *propitiation* in the Word of God is used in the context of *jurisprudence*. In other words, it is a word used to describe *divine justice*. A just judge cannot be just if he does not require the sentence he places upon the guilty one to be executed exactly as he demands. God cannot merely *forgive* the debt of the transgression of sin. If a sinner pays for his own sin it means he must be eternally separated from God and suffer eternal torment in Hell. God must *satisfy* the debt by executing the sentence of eternal separation from Him in the body of His Incarnate Son while He hung on Calvary's Cross. We may never fully understand what took place in the *three hours of darkness* while Jesus was on the Cross (Matthew 27:45-46; Luke 23:24-26), but we can know with surety that God's eternal wrath upon sin was satisfied during that period. **There can be no pardon apart from propitiation**. God satisfied His penalty upon sin by becoming a man, living a sinless life, and dying in the place of sinners to pay their sin debt (Romans 5:8).

Understanding the propitiation of God through the substitutionary death of Christ Jesus opens the door for our potential understanding of the gift of justification to the believing/trusting sinner. We have all heard the simple definition of justification as being *just as if I never sinned*. Although this definition is *simple*, it is also *superficial*. It is *superficial* because justification has to do with the *gift* of God-kind righteousness to the believing sinner. Before Christ "finished" propitiating God, God-kind righteousness was *imputed* to the believing sinner. Faith was "counted to him for righteousness" (Genesis 15:6; Romans 4:1-7). After Christ "finished" propitiating God, God-kind righteousness was *imparted* to the believing sinner through the impartation of the indwelling Spirit of God. The "divine nature" is the indwelling Holy Spirit of God *imparted* to all believers the moment they call upon Jesus to save them. Thereby, the believing sinner literally possesses the righteousness of God. Therefore, there is an expectation that accompanies justification to living godly.

> [1] Simon Peter, a servant and an apostle of Jesus Christ, to them that have obtained like precious faith with us through the righteousness of God and our Saviour Jesus Christ: [2] Grace and peace be multiplied unto you through the knowledge of God, and of Jesus our Lord, [3] **According as his divine power hath given unto us all things that *pertain* unto life and godliness, through the knowledge of him that hath called us to glory and virtue:** [4] Whereby are given unto us exceeding great and precious promises: that by these ye might be partakers {*partner*} of the divine nature, having escaped the corruption that is in the world through lust (II Peter 1:1-4).

A simple way to explain these truths to someone is to explain that God requires a person to be both sinless and as righteous as God is righteous in order to enter God's presence. Such a statement will immediately get a person's attention bringing them to an understanding of the hopelessness of trying to pursue salvation based upon their own merit. From this position of desperation, a proper explanation of propitiation and justification will solve both impossible problems for sinners, helping them understand that salvation is a gift offered by God's grace and received through faith.

> [1] Brethren, my heart's desire and prayer to God for Israel is, that they might be saved. [2] For I bear them record that they

have a zeal of God, but not according to knowledge {*full discernment or complete understanding*}. [3] For they being ignorant of God's righteousness {*God-kind righteous*ness}, and going about to establish their own righteousness {*man-kind righteousness*}, have not submitted themselves unto the righteousness of God. [4] For Christ *is* the end of the law for righteousness to every one that believeth (Romans 10:1-4).

There are those who teach that Romans 10:1-13 is just for leading Jews to Christ. They will teach that *only believing* is necessary for everyone except Jews. Of course, this is absolute foolishness. Jews do not get saved any differently than any other sinner. In fact, the Epistle to the Romans is addressed to Roman (Gentile) Christians.

We can find a *straight-line pattern* in Romans 10:1-13 of God's expected responses to an understanding of the details of the Gospel of Jesus Christ. In Romans 10:9-13, we find three of the five verbs defining a faith decision to be "born again." In all, a saving *faith decision* is actually five decisions following one another in consecutive order.

1. **Believe** in thine heart
2. **Confess** with thine mouth
3. **Call** on the Name

[9] That if thou shalt confess with thy mouth the Lord Jesus, and shalt believe in thine heart that God hath raised him from the dead, thou shalt be saved. [10] For with the heart man believeth unto righteousness {*imparted*}; and with the mouth confession is made unto salvation. [11] For the scripture saith, Whosoever believeth on him shall not be ashamed. [12] For there is no difference between the Jew and the Greek: for the same Lord over all is rich unto all that call upon him. [13] For whosoever shall call upon the name of the Lord shall be saved. [14] How then shall they call on him in whom they have not believed? and how shall they believe in him of whom they have not heard? and how shall they hear without a preacher? [15] And how shall they preach, except they be sent? as it is written, How beautiful are the feet of them that

> preach the gospel of peace, and bring glad tidings of good things! [16] But they have not all obeyed the gospel. For Esaias saith, Lord, who hath believed our report? [17] So then faith *cometh* by hearing, and hearing by the word of God (Romans 10:9-17).

There is considerable theological depth in the statement of Paul to the question of the Philippian jailer in Acts 16:31, "Sirs, what must I **do** to be saved?" There Paul says, "believe on the Lord Jesus Christ." "Believe" is the verb describing the **action** upon the subject "the Lord Jesus Christ." To understand the meaning of the word *believe*, we must return to the Hebrew word *'aman* (aw-man'). The original Hebrew word for *faith*, or *believe*, is Hebrew word *'aman* (aw-man'). To affirm faith in a promise of God or an affirmation of truth proclaimed in the word of God was done so by an *Amen* exclamation.

> For all the promises of God in him *are* yea, and in him Amen, unto the glory of God by us (II Corinthians 1:20).

To *believe* is more than a mere intellectual assent to the facts of the Gospel. The basic idea in the word *believe* is to identify with a *certainty*. Therefore, the implication of the word *believe* means *to rest* in the accomplishments of Jesus Christ on our behalf in His finished work of redemption as a *certainty*.

Of course, Jesus is "the Lord Jesus Christ." To "believe on the Lord Jesus Christ" presumes an understanding of the terms "Lord" and "Christ" and what these terms mean as they are related to the Person called Jesus. We have many who profess to "believe on the Lord Jesus Christ" without ever understanding what these terms mean. It is the function of the soul winner to insure the person being brought to faith in Jesus Christ understands these terms and believes in the Person to whom these terms refer. The doctrines of propitiation and justification are meaningless apart from the meaning of the terms "the Lord Jesus Christ." In other words, propitiation and justification could never have been accomplished apart from the miraculous redemptive work of the incarnate, sinless, Jehovah God revealed to us by the terms "the Lord Jesus Christ." The sole condition for the impartation of the righteousness of Christ to the sinner (justification) is to "believe on the Lord Jesus Christ."

> [16] For I am not ashamed of the gospel of Christ: for it is the power of God unto salvation to every one that believeth; to the Jew first, and also to the Greek. [17] For therein is the righteousness of God revealed from {*saving*} faith to {*living*} faith: as it is written, The just shall live by faith (Romans 1:16-17).

The doctrine of justification, in conjunction with the doctrine of propitiation, teaches us how God can provide salvation without compromising His standard of righteousness in the Law. According to Romans 3:26, God is both "just" and the "Justifier." God is "just" because His wrath and condemnation upon sin has been satisfied. God did this without compromising His justice or holiness through the substitutionary death of His incarnate sinless Son. He is the "Justifier" in that His mercy can be shown in grace as He restores a believer to a position in righteousness before Him.

God is "just" because His justice demands the adjudication of His death sentence for sin. God is the "Justifier" in that His grace pays the "wages of sin" in the substitute sacrifice of Christ.

Years ago, a family by the name of Rosenberg were tried for treason as Russian spies against the U.S.A. The judge who proceeded over the trial was Judge Kaufman. The Rosenbergs were convicted of treason after a long and bitter trial and then sentenced to death. In his summation, the Rosenberg's lawyer passionately and emotionally pleaded with the court for justice. Judge Kaufman calmly replied, "The court has given you what you ask for – justice! What you really want is mercy, but that is something this court has no right to give you."

The Law has no right or ability to give mercy or grace. The Law gives what the lawbreaker deserves. This is universally true. The Law gives justice. God incarnate brings grace and mercy to the Law. In grace and mercy, God takes the death sentence of sin upon Himself and pays it for us.

This new standard of righteousness is shown to the world by the "faith" (*faithfulness*) of Jesus Christ (Romans 3:22).

Salvation is never based upon what we do (or do not do). The foundation of salvation is solely what Christ has done on our behalf. Christ's faithful obedience to everything the Law demands is a full revelation of the righteousness of God. Because Jesus was faithful in fulfilling every aspect of the Law, He can give to us His righteousness as the new Federal Head ("last Adam") of the New Creation. This is known as the *doctrine of imputation.*

> 9 For we are labourers together with God: ye {*plural and therefore collectively*} are God's husbandry, *ye are* God's building {*the local church at Corinth*}. 10 According to the grace of God which is given unto me, **as a wise masterbuilder, I have laid the foundation**, and another buildeth thereon. But let every man take heed how he buildeth thereupon. 11 **For other foundation can no man lay than that is laid, which is Jesus Christ.** 12 Now if any man build upon this foundation gold, silver, precious stones, wood, hay, stubble; 13 Every man's work shall be made manifest: for the day shall declare it, because it shall be revealed by fire; and the fire shall try every man's work of what sort it is. 14 If any man's work abide which he hath built thereupon, he shall receive a reward. 15 If any man's work shall be burned, he shall suffer loss: but he himself shall be saved; yet so as by fire (I Corinthians 3:9-15).

This "righteousness of God" comes "unto all" *in* Jesus Christ. In other words, God's righteousness is made available to "whosoever will" through the faithfulness of Jesus Christ. The "righteousness of God" comes "upon all them that believe" (Romans 3:22). This is God's consistent truth throughout Scripture.

> 5 But to him that worketh not, but **believeth on him that justifieth the ungodly**, his faith is counted for righteousness. 6 Even as David also describeth the blessedness of the man, **unto whom God imputeth righteousness without works** (Romans 4:5-6).

> For Christ *is* the end of the law for righteousness **to every one that believeth** (Romans 10:4).

> And be found in him, not having mine own righteousness, which is of the law, but that which is through the faith of Christ, **the righteousness which is of God by faith** (Philippians 3:9).

"For there is no difference" (Romans 3:22b). Everyone needs God's righteousness given to them as a gift, because everyone has sinned (Romans 3:23). Therefore, no one can ever be as righteous as God is even if he could live sinless for the rest of his life.

Justification is a free gift of God's grace because righteousness is imputed "freely" (Romans 3:24).

Justification, as the result of the imputation of God's righteousness, is a *free gift*. Justification is expensive to God. It is free to us. Justification comes to the believer as a free gift "through the redemption that is in Jesus Christ."

Eternal separation from God (death) is the price of redemption. Death was the price paid for our justification. "Where is boasting then?" (Romans 3:27). Who has some claim to goodness or righteousness before God? Who can demand justice from God without knowing he will receive condemnation? There is no "boasting" about righteousness before God. Boasting is excluded. Boasting is *shut out*. The kind of thinking that lays claim to God-kind righteousness based on human merit. This kind of thinking closes the door of heaven against the person thinking he has achieved the kind of righteousness with which God is satisfied.

The concluding statement is found in Romans 3:28; "a man is justified by faith" totally apart from keeping the Law or personal attempts at righteousness. When Romans 3:23 says we "come short of the glory of God," God means none deserve God's glory except they that are as righteous as is God. God's grace provides His righteousness as a gift and ultimately the redemption of the body in glorification. Glorification is the ultimate act of justification to a state of perfect and practical sanctification before God.

[29] For whom he did foreknow, he also did **predestinate *to be* conformed to the image of his Son**, that he might be the firstborn among many brethren. [30] Moreover whom he did predestinate, them he also called: and whom he called, them he also justified: and **whom he justified, them he also glorified** (Romans 8:29-30).

The central message of the Gospel is the propitiation of God, not the justification of man. Propitiation is the satisfaction of God's righteous demand for justice. The justification of man is a byproduct of the propitiation of God.

The righteousness of God that is revealed in the Gospel is that righteousness which becomes incarnate in Jesus Christ and righteously pays the "wages of sin" (which is the death sentence). This was accomplished for all mankind by Jesus being our sinless substitute on the Cross of Calvary. The Gospel is not about how righteous or religious a person can be, but about how God's love sent His Son from the glories of eternity to die the death of a condemned criminal to satisfy God's justice (death sentence).

When propitiation is the central message of the Gospel, *satisfying* God's righteousness is the focus (not *attaining* to God's righteousness, which can never be done).

> But we are all as an unclean *thing*, and all our righteousnesses *are* as filthy rags; and we all do fade as a leaf; and our iniquities, like the wind, have taken us away (Isaiah 64:6).

> [10] As it is written, There is none righteous, no, not one: [11]
> There is none that understandeth, there is none that seeketh
> after God. [12] They are all gone out of the way, they are
> together become unprofitable; there is none that doeth good,
> no, not one. [13] Their throat *is* an open sepulchre; with their
> tongues they have used deceit; the poison of asps *is* under
> their lips: [14] Whose mouth *is* full of cursing and bitterness:
> [15] Their feet *are* swift to shed blood: [16] Destruction and
> misery *are* in their ways: [17] And the way of peace have they
> not known: [18] There is no fear of God before their eyes
> (Romans 3:10-18).

God's righteousness is revealed in the Gospel "from {*saving*} faith to {*living*} faith" (Romans 1:17). It is the faithfulness ("faith") of Jesus Christ in obedience to the will of God that reveals to us a God so righteous He would send His own Son to the Cross of Calvary to pay the wages of sin rather than compromise His righteousness in any way. "From faith to faith" deals with the imputation of God's righteous to the person who trusts in Christ and what He did to propitiate God's wrath upon sin. This is expanded upon in Romans 3:22.

> Even the righteousness of God *which is* by faith of Jesus Christ unto all and upon all them that believe: for there is no difference (Romans 3:22).

"By faith of Jesus Christ" should be "by the faithfulness of Jesus Christ." Jesus was faithful in doing what He was sent to do. Therefore, God was propitiated and the believing sinner can be justified and freed from the condemnation of sin. The believing sinner is also *declared* righteous in Jesus Christ. Through the faithfulness of Jesus Christ to the will of God and the substitutionary death of the Cross, Jesus made available "unto all and upon all them that believe" the righteousness of God which justifies the believing sinner.

"The just (justified) shall live by faith(fullness)" (Romans 1:17). This is quoted from Habakkuk 2:4. We need to understand its meaning from that context.

> Behold, his soul *which* is lifted up is not upright in him: but the just shall live by his faith (Habakkuk 2:4).

The word translated "just" is from the Hebrew word *tsaddiyq* (tsad-deek'), referring to a righteous person because he has been justified and vindicated by God. The word translated "faith" is from the Hebrew word *'emuwnah* (em-oo-naw') and refers to a person's fidelity to truth and steadfastness in it.

The intent of the statement "the just shall live by faith" is that a person saved and justified by faith in Messiah and His propitiatory work is obligated to live a life of faithfulness. A person is not saved by living righteously, but if he is saved he is obligated to live according to the principles and precepts of the Word of God. The "just" are obligated to live righteously in that they are declared righteous in Jesus Christ.

Questions for Discussion

1. Discuss why it is essential to understand the following three terms before a person can rest/believe in them.

   A. The **vicarious** nature of the death, burial, and resurrection of Jesus
   B. The **propitiation** of God's wrath through the death, burial, and resurrection of Jesus
   C. The gift of **justification** through faith in the death, burial, and resurrection of Jesus

2. Discuss how God was *propitiated* through the *vicarious offering* of His Son at Calvary.

3. Discuss the meaning of the word *propitiation* in the Word of God is as it is used in the context of *jurisprudence*.

4. Explain how *understanding* God being *propitiated* by the *vicarious offering* of Jesus and God *gifting the righteousness* of Jesus to the believing sinner solves the problem of God requiring a person to be both sinless and as righteous as God is righteous to enter God's presence.

5. Discuss why it is important to understand that the *propitiation of God's wrath* is the central message of the Gospel rather than *the justification of the sinner*.

Chapter Five

The Journey to Confessing Christ

While sitting in a crowed restaurant with a new acquaintance, I bowed my head and gave God thanks for our meal. The person with me was obviously uncomfortable about public prayer in a public place and with me mentioning the name of Jesus out loud. We would expect such discomfort from lost and worldly people. However, such discomfort is also commonplace among professing Christians. The Postmodern, secular, *politically correct* culture seeks to silence the public voice of Christians, forcing them to speak only of Christ behind the closed doors of their churches or homes.

There are a few *whispering believers* recorded in the Bible. If we read the accounts of their lives, we discover they overcame their fears and were willing to publicly identify themselves with Jesus Christ. Dr. Nicodemus of John chapter three was one of these individuals. We will see a tremendous transition in his life when he finally decides it is not worth denying Jesus Christ and living a lie, even if it cost him his life. Ultimately, that is a decision each of us must make one day.

> 1 There was a man of the Pharisees, named Nicodemus, a ruler of the Jews: 2 **The same came to Jesus by night**, and said unto him, Rabbi, **we know** that thou art a teacher come from God: for no man can do these miracles that thou doest, except God be with him. 3 Jesus answered and said unto him, Verily, verily, I say unto thee, Except a man be born again, he cannot see the kingdom of God. 4 Nicodemus saith unto him, How can a man be born when he is old? can he enter the second time into his mother's womb, and be born? 5 Jesus answered, Verily, verily, I say unto thee, Except a man be born of water and *of* the Spirit, he cannot enter into the kingdom of God. 6 That which is born of the flesh is flesh; and that which is born of the Spirit is spirit. 7 Marvel not that I said unto thee, Ye must be born again. 8 The wind bloweth where it listeth, and thou hearest the sound thereof, but canst

> not tell whence it cometh, and whither it goeth: so is every one that is born of the Spirit. 9 Nicodemus answered and said unto him, How can these things be? 10 Jesus answered and said unto him, **Art thou a master of Israel, and knowest not these things**? 11 Verily, verily, I say unto thee, We speak that we do know, and testify that we have seen; and **ye receive not our witness**. 12 If I have told you earthly things, and ye believe not, how shall ye believe, if I tell you *of* heavenly things? 13 And no man hath ascended up to heaven, but he that came down from heaven, *even* the Son of man which is in heaven. 14 And as Moses lifted up the serpent in the wilderness, even so must the Son of man be lifted up: 15 That whosoever believeth in him should not perish, but have eternal life. 16 For God so loved the world, that he gave his only begotten Son, that whosoever believeth in him should not perish, but have everlasting life. 17 For God sent not his Son into the world to condemn the world; but that the world through him might be saved. 18 He that believeth on him is not condemned: but he that believeth not is condemned already, because he hath not believed in the name of the only begotten Son of God. 19 And this is the condemnation, that light is come into the world, and **men loved darkness rather than light**, because their deeds were evil. 20 For every one that doeth evil hateth the light, neither cometh to the light, lest his deeds should be reproved. 21 But **he that doeth truth cometh to the light, that his deeds may be made manifest, that they are wrought in God** (John 3:1-21).

The life of a *whispering believer* is a lie. He privately professes to be one thing, while publicly being silent. **In John 3:1-2, Dr. Nicodemus comes to Jesus by night. This fact is important if we are going to understand much of what Christ says to him.** Dr. Nicodemus purposely waited until after dark to seek out Jesus. Nicodemus was a Pharisee and a member of the Seventy. These were seventy ruling elders called the Sanhedrin, which were the most influential group of Jews in Israel.

According to John 3:10, Nicodemus was commonly known as *"the"* teacher of Israel. *(The definite article is present in the Greek text.)* He was very well known. **In John 3:2, we find this**

very famous ruler of the Jews sneaking in the shadows of darkness, carefully looking over his shoulder to be sure no one sees him. Nicodemus was grateful for the darkness because it hid him. It kept anyone from knowing he was going to see Jesus. He was afraid if someone saw him, he would lose his position of power and respect.

We must question what really is at stake because of Nicodemus' fear of being identified with Christ. Is the most important thing at stake the position of Nicodemus? Or, is it most important that someone might not be saved because Nicodemus is afraid of being identified with Christ? It is this latter issue to which Christ speaks in John 3:19. Nicodemus **was *almost* a believer.** Satan used fear as a tool to keep Nicodemus sneaking around in the darkness and living a lie. Christ was telling Nicodemus that fear of being identified with Christ was a central reason why people continue to be condemned. Salvation was freely available and Nicodemus, a spiritual leader of Israel, was afraid to publicly proclaim how to get it.

Doers of truth live openly for Christ (John 3:21).

This is another confrontation of Nicodemus' hypocrisy. He was a teacher of truth. Christ differentiates between teaching truth and living truth. "He that **doeth** (not "teaches") truth cometh to the light (out into the open where everyone can see)." Christ expects those who are genuinely saved to be public about that salvation. Christ expects those who are really saved to be willing to publicly stand with Him where everyone can see.

> [7] For God hath not given us the spirit of fear; but of power, and of love, and of a sound mind. [8] Be not thou therefore ashamed of the testimony of our Lord, nor of me his prisoner: but be thou partaker of the afflictions of the gospel according to the power of God (II Timothy 1:7-8).

Reading John 7:45-52, we begin to see Nicodemus overcoming his fear.

> [45] Then came the officers to the chief priests and Pharisees; and they said unto them, Why have ye not brought him? [46]

The officers answered, Never man spake like this man. [47] Then answered them the Pharisees, Are ye also deceived? [48] **Have any of the rulers or of the Pharisees believed on him?** [49] But this people who knoweth not the law are cursed. [50] **Nicodemus saith unto them, (he that came to Jesus by night, being one of them,)** [51] **Doth our law judge any man, before it hear him, and know what he doeth?** [52] They answered and said unto him, **Art thou also of Galilee?** Search, and look: for out of Galilee ariseth no prophet (John 7:45-52).

The question of John 7:48 is essentially, "has anyone important (like us) believed on him?" Then one voice out of these seventy rulers speaks. It is Nicodemus throwing away his crutches of fear and taking his first baby steps out of the darkness and into the light (verses 50 and 51).

Did the other members of the Sanhedrin all become believers because Nicodemus came stumbling out of the darkness (verse 52)? No! But that is not the important thing here. Nicodemus took his first step to free himself from his fear by this small attempt to stand up for Christ. It was a baby step of faith that would refuse to allow fear to keep him hiding in the darkness. Nicodemus began to put justice and righteousness first. He became a doer of truth and stuck his head out into the light.

Was it true that none of the other rulers believed Jesus was Messiah as John 7:48 says? The fact is that many of the seventy believed, but they were also *whispering believers*. Read John 12:42-43.

[42] Nevertheless among the chief rulers also **many believed on him**; but because of the Pharisees **they did not confess *him***, lest they should be put out of the synagogue: [43] **For they loved the praise of men more than the praise of God** (John 12:42-43).

They believed Jesus was Messiah, but feared to publicly confess Him because of fear of rejection. Were they saved (remember Romans 10:8-11)?

> [8] But what saith it? The word is nigh thee, even in thy mouth, and in thy heart: that is, the word of faith, which we preach; [9] That **if thou shalt confess with thy mouth the Lord Jesus**, <u>and</u> shalt believe in thine heart that God hath raised him from the dead, thou shalt be saved. [10] For with the heart man believeth unto righteousness; and with the mouth confession is made unto salvation. [11] For the scripture saith, Whosoever believeth on him shall not be ashamed (Romans 10:8-11).

The Bible says you must *"confess... <u>and</u> believe."* These men were *only* believers. They loved the praise and acceptance of men (John 12:43). They were unwilling to publicly identify themselves as believers in Jesus. Peer pressure kept them from getting saved.

Nicodemus' story doesn't end in John chapter seven. Read John 19:38-39.

> [38] And after this Joseph of Arimathaea, being a disciple of Jesus, but **secretly for fear of the Jews**, besought Pilate that he might take away the body of Jesus: and Pilate gave *him* leave. He came therefore, and took the body of Jesus. [39] And there came also Nicodemus, **which at the first** came to Jesus by night, and brought a mixture of myrrh and aloes, about an hundred pound *weight* (John 19:38-39).

Two former *whispering believers* step fully out of the shadows and into the light. Joseph of Arimathea was also a *whispering believer* in Jesus. After he and Nicodemus saw what Jesus was willing to do for them at Calvary, there was no more hiding in the shadows.

It is difficult for me to believe how anyone who truly understands and believes what the Son of God was willing to do in the incarnation, crucifixion, and resurrection could possibly be silent about that. The eternal Son of God was willing to eternally become a man to save our sin loving souls.

From **the moment of conception, the Son of God has eternally identified Himself with man by becoming a man for all eternity.** How can someone understand that and still be unwilling to pay whatever price necessary to be identified with

Him. Nicodemus and Joseph of Arimathea understood it. It is almost as if they came running out of the shadows to identify themselves with Jesus.

In the first century A.D., there was a wealthy member of the Sanhedrin named Nicodemus ben Gorion. He was the brother of Josephus, the famous Jewish historian. If this is the Nicodemus of the Gospel of John, he lost his wealth and position because of his public identification with Jesus. He was willing to give up the power and prestige of this world for one simple thing. He wanted His Savior to know he loved Him more than anything or anyone else in the world, even if it meant the loss of everything he had.

> For what is a man profited, if he shall gain the whole world, and lose his own soul? or what shall a man give in exchange for his soul (Matthew 16:26)?

Questions for Discussion

1. Discuss why being a *whispering believer* is a contradiction against what God describes in Romans 10:9 with the words "*confess with thy mouth.*"

2. Discuss why and in what way the life of a *whispering believer* is a lie.

3. Discuss the transition in Nicodemus's life that takes place in John 7:45-52 showing that Nicodemus is beginning to escape his fear of man to identify with Jesus as the Christ.

4. Discuss what is revealed in John 12:42-43 about why other members of the Sanhedrin were *only believers* and therefore still lost.

5. Discuss what John 19:38-39 reveals about Nicodemus and Joseph of Arimathea showing a change in their willingness to publicly confess Jesus to be the Christ and identifying with Him.

Learning to Lead

Chapter Six

Confessing Jesus as Lord

Romans chapter ten is at the heart of three parenthetical chapters of Romans that deal nationally and dispensationally with Israel. Romans 10:1-13 gives specific instructions for what defines a faith decision for Jews to "be saved." The nation of Israel had been led astray and deceived by the very priesthood that God had ordained to preserve His Word through teaching and through practice. The priesthood had perverted the purpose of the Mosaic Covenant, the Law; by teaching that Law keeping could produce the righteousness necessary to *salvation.*

In other words, the nation of Israel had been deceived by their priesthood into believing that they could be "justified" by "the works of the Law." In Galatians 2:16, the Apostle Paul clearly and unequivocally states, "Knowing that a man is not justified by the works of the law, but by the faith of Jesus Christ, even we have believed in Jesus Christ, that we might be justified by the faith of Christ, and not by the works of the law: for by the works of the law shall no flesh be justified." This is the substance of Romans 10:1-13 that defines a faith response to the finished work of redemption in the Person of Jesus the Christ.

> [1] Brethren, my heart's desire and prayer to God for Israel is,
> that they might be saved. [2] For I bear them record that they
> have a zeal of God, but not according to knowledge. [3] For
> they being ignorant of God's righteousness, and going about
> to establish their own righteousness, have not submitted
> themselves unto the righteousness of God. [4] For Christ *is* the
> end of the law for righteousness to every one that believeth.
> [5] For Moses describeth the righteousness which is of the law,
> That the man which doeth those things shall live by them. [6]
> But the righteousness which is of faith speaketh on this wise,
> Say not in thine heart, Who shall ascend into heaven? (that
> is, to bring Christ down *from above*:) [7] Or, Who shall
> descend into the deep? (that is, to bring up Christ again from
> the dead.) [8] But what saith it? The word is nigh thee, *even* in

thy mouth, and in thy heart: that is, the word of faith, which we preach; [9] That if thou shalt **confess** with thy mouth the Lord Jesus, and shalt **believe** in thine heart that God hath raised him from the dead, thou shalt be saved. [10] For with the heart man believeth unto righteousness; and with the mouth confession is made unto salvation. [11] For the scripture saith, Whosoever believeth on him shall not be ashamed. [12] For there is no difference between the Jew and the Greek: for the same Lord over all is rich unto all that call upon him. [13] For whosoever shall call upon the name of the Lord shall be saved (Romans 10:1-11).

In this Romans 10:1-11, Paul quotes from the books of the Law to reestablish God's intended purpose of the Law. From these few quotes, it becomes obvious that the priesthood of Israel had perverted the purpose of the Law to say people could achieve righteousness satisfactory to God for a kind of *self-righteous justification.*

As Romans 10:4 says, the purpose of the Law was to point to the need of a Saviour Who would die vicariously for the sins of the people. Christ, the Promised Anointed One, is Jehovah incarnate in a human body by being born of a virgin. This was announced as a fulfillment of Isaiah 7:14 in Matthew 1:22-23.

[22] Now all this was done, that it might be fulfilled which was spoken of the Lord by the prophet, saying, [23] Behold, a virgin shall be with child, and shall bring forth a son, and they shall call his name Emmanuel, which being interpreted is, God with us (Matthew 1:22-23).

The word "end" in Romans 10:4 is from the Greek word *telos* (tel′-os). The word refers to a *point aimed at.* Therefore, Christ is the *point aimed at* in the Law. No human being could ever achieve the extreme degree of righteousness to which the Law *aimed at.* Christ did. Therefore, He met every obligation of the Law vicariously for all of humanity.

[17] Think not that I am come to destroy the law, or the prophets: I am not come to destroy, but to fulfil. [18] For verily

> I say unto you, Till heaven and earth pass, one jot or one tittle shall in no wise pass from the law, till all be fulfilled (Matthew 5:17-18).

The word "fulfilled" in Matthew 5:18 is from the Greek word *pleroo* (play-ro'-o), which means *to cram full.* Jesus vicariously met every minute detail of the Law, even the spirit of the Law. This truth is absolutely critical to understanding why belief in His resurrection (Romans 10:9) is essential to the Gospel and to a believer's salvation.

> For he hath made him *to be* sin for us, who knew no sin; that we might be **made** the righteousness of God in him (II Corinthians 5:21).

Paul refers to what Moses recorded in Leviticus 18:5 by the statement in Romans 10:5-7 – "[5] For Moses describeth the righteousness which is of the law, That the man which doeth those things shall live by them. [6] But the righteousness which is of faith speaketh on this wise, Say not in thine heart, Who shall ascend into heaven? (that is, to bring Christ down *from above*:) [7] Or, Who shall descend into the deep? (that is, to bring up Christ again from the dead.)." Leviticus 18:5 was God's statement regarding the Mosaic Covenant. The nation of Israel accepted God's conditions for blessings under the Mosaic Covenant. However, almost every generation failed to keep the "statutes, and judgments" of God, thereby bringing God's chastisement upon the nation of Israel.

> [1] And the LORD spake unto Moses, saying, [2] Speak unto the children of Israel, and say unto them, I am the LORD your God. [3] After the doings of the land of Egypt, wherein ye dwelt, shall ye not do: and after the doings of the land of Canaan, whither I bring you, shall ye not do: neither shall ye walk in their ordinances. [4] Ye shall do my judgments, and keep mine ordinances, to walk therein: I *am* the LORD your God. [5] Ye shall therefore keep my statutes, and my judgments: which if a man do, he shall live in them: I *am* the LORD (Leviticus 18:1-5).

The words "he shall live in them" simply mean that a man would be blessed temporally and spiritually if he lived within the boundaries of God's "statutes" and "judgments." This statement does not refer to *eternal life*. The Law was given for *relational* purposes, not *salvational* purposes.

In Romans 10:8, Paul declares the ultimate correction of the purpose of the Law – "But what saith it {*meaning the righteousness that comes through faith – see 10:6*}? The word is nigh thee, *even* in thy mouth, and in thy heart: that is, the word of faith, which we preach." The two uses of "word" in Romans 10:6 are from the Greek word *rhema* (hray'-mah). The word means *utterance* or *proclamation.* Paul is not referring to the written Word of God. He was referring to the Word of God *proclaimed, explained,* and *understood* in the heart.

The simple answer to the condemnation of the Law due to humanity's utter failure to keep it is the proclamation of faith in the promised Messiah. The *good news* is God's solution to man's dilemma. Humanity is hopelessly lost in sin. The condemnation and penalty of sin must be remitted. Yet the Law of God still required the fulfillment of the righteous requirements of the Law. Otherwise God would be deemed unjust for merely releasing a sinner from his deserved penalty. Paul already dealt with this in Romans chapter three.

> 19 Now we know that what things soever the law saith, it saith
> to them who are under the law: that every mouth may be
> stopped, and all the world may become guilty before God. 20
> Therefore by the deeds of the law there shall no flesh be
> justified in his sight: for by the law *is* the knowledge of sin.
> 21 But now the righteousness of God without the law is
> manifested, being witnessed by the law and the prophets; 22
> Even the righteousness of God *which is* by faith of Jesus
> Christ unto all and upon all them that believe: for there is no
> difference: 23 For all have sinned, and come short of the glory
> of God; 24 Being justified freely by his grace through the
> redemption that is in Christ Jesus: 25 Whom God hath set
> forth *to be* a propitiation through faith in his blood, to declare
> his righteousness for the remission of sins that are past,
> through the forbearance of God; 26 To declare, *I say*, at this

> time his righteousness: that he might be just, and the justifier of him which believeth in Jesus. [27] Where *is* boasting then? It is excluded. By what law? of works? Nay: but by the law of faith. [28] Therefore we conclude that a man is justified by faith without the deeds of the law (Romans 3:19-28).

Apart from the *proclamation, explanation,* and *understanding* of the Gospel in the death, burial, and resurrection of Jesus the Christ, no one could understand how faith brings *God-kind righteousness* to sinners. The *proclamation, explanation,* and *understanding* of the Gospel were exemplified by Christ in the parable of the sower, the soils, and the seed (Galatians 3:16) in Matthew 13:1-23.

> [13] Therefore speak I to them in parables: because they seeing see not; and hearing they hear not, neither do they understand. [14] And in them is fulfilled the prophecy of Esaias, which saith, By hearing ye shall hear, and shall not understand; and seeing ye shall see, and shall not perceive: [15] For this people's heart is waxed gross, and *their* ears are dull of hearing, and their eyes they have closed; lest at any time they should see with *their* eyes, and hear with *their* ears, and should understand with *their* heart, and should be converted, and I should heal them (Matthew 13:13-15).

The main point of the parable is the explanation of the purpose of the incarnation of Jehovah in the Person of Jesus. Unless a person understands the main redemptive purpose of the incarnation of Jehovah, that person will have *deaf ears* to the Gospel, no *understanding* of the Gospel, and *spiritual blindness* to the Gospel message. Such a person "shall not perceive" or be enabled to understand his need of a Saviour. Understanding *with the heart* is essential to *conversion* or being spiritually "born again."

Paul is quoting from Deuteronomy 30:11-14 in Romans 10:8. This is important because the use of this Mosaic Covenant text is explaining to the Jews that what Paul was teaching was not some new doctrine. Deuteronomy 30:1-14 describes the "blessing and the curse" in the Old Covenant. Deuteronomy 30:1-10 details the regathering of the nation of Israel after their complete repentance – "*and* if thou turn unto the LORD thy God with all thine heart, and with all thy soul" (Deuteronomy 30:10). **The first ten verses of Deuteronomy chapter thirty establish that faith in the Messiah must be preceded by complete repentance from all practices contrary to the absolutes of the Mosaic Covenant.** The intent of Deuteronomy 30:11-14 is that although national Israel had moved far from God in their sinful practices and the nation was far from the Promised Land due to God's chastisement, restoration and reconciliation were only as far away as were repentance and faith in their hearts. This is the context that Paul brings to Romans 10:9-13. These Old Testament verses are extremely important to understanding the Jewish context of Romans 10:9-13.

> [11]For this commandment which I command thee this day, it *is* not hidden from thee, neither *is* it far off. [12] It *is* not in heaven, that thou shouldest say, Who shall go up for us to heaven, and bring it unto us, that we may hear it, and do it? [13] Neither *is* it beyond the sea, that thou shouldest say, Who shall go over the sea for us, and bring it unto us, that we may hear it, and do it? [14] But the word *is* very nigh unto thee, in thy mouth, and in thy heart, that thou mayest do it (Deuteronomy 30:11-14).

The KJV translators have ended Romans 10:8 with a semicolon to show us the connection between two transitional phrases that are closely related. In other words, "the word of faith, which we preach" is going to be defined in Romans 10:9. Romans 10:9 is then explained in more detail in Romans 10:10-13. This is critically important in that the "faith" of Romans 10:8 is defined by the three verbs of Romans 10:9-13 –believe, confess, and call (repentance having been already established by the quote from Deuteronomy chapter thirty).

> That if thou shalt confess with thy mouth the Lord Jesus, and shalt believe in thine heart that God hath raised him from the dead, thou shalt be saved (Romans 10:9).

The words "with thy mouth" and "in thine heart" correspond with God's solution given in Deuteronomy 30:14 – "But the word *is* very nigh unto thee, in thy mouth, and in thy heart, that thou mayest do it" (Deuteronomy 30:11-14). The understanding of Deuteronomy 30:14 was that these Jews were very near to salvation, but not yet there. The Jews thought they were near to *self-justification* because they thought they approached *self-righteo*usness in the works of the Law. In Romans 10:9, Paul clarifies that the "word" that brought them near to true justification was the proclamation of justification through faith in the Substitute. Although this "word of faith" was in their hearts and in their mouths, they needed to declare outwardly that same "word of faith." **In other words, "the word of faith" must be expressed in a tangible way.**

Obviously, to "believe in thine heart" that justification comes through faith in the Substitute required repenting from trusting in their works of self-righteousness. Self-justification before God is a foolish notion. How can someone who begins as a sinner (Romans 5:12) somehow become righteous by his own efforts? **Therefore, to "believe in thine heart" relates to two objective decisions.** First, there must be an understanding of the objective facts of the Gospel in the Substitute.

Understanding the *purpose* of Christ (Jehovah's incarnation in Jesus) is the ground for understanding the Gospel and a person's complete dependence upon the redemptive work of Christ. Show me a man who is not serious about living for Christ and I will show you a man who does not understand his redemption or the price paid to give it to him. This is the substance of the parable of the *sower, soils*, and *seed* (Galatians 3:16) in Matthew 13:1-23. Only a proper understanding of the objective facts of the Gospel through a thorough explanation of those facts can result in repentance of "dead works." Only a proper understanding of the objective facts of the Gospel, through a thorough explanation of those facts, can result in a person fully resting in the finished work of redemption provided by the righteous life, death, burial, and the resurrection of Jesus.

Therefore, such faith would be expressed in the complete abandonment of the "works of the Law" as means of justification before God. Such faith would be expressed in the complete abandonment of the sacrifices of the Mosaic Covenant. Such faith would be expressed in the complete abandonment of the need for the Levitical priesthood of the Mosaic Covenant. If one truly believed "in thine heart" that justification was in the accomplished realities of the substitutionary life, death, burial, and resurrection of the incarnate Jehovah, why would such a person continue in practices that denied that finished work?

Secondly, the "word" of faith that was "in thy mouth" per Deuteronomy 30:14 must be *verbally expressed.* The "word of faith" is the proclamation that Jesus is Jehovah incarnate. Jesus is the Substitute provided "by grace" through which faith provides justification to the believing sinner. Therefore, there must be a public declaration, or *confession,* of faith that Jesus is Jehovah incarnate. This *confession* is expressed by the phrase "the Lord Jesus" in Romans 10:9 and 10. The expanse of such a *confession* is expressed by the Apostle Peter in Matthew 16:16.

> 13 When Jesus came into the coasts of Caesarea Philippi, he asked his disciples, saying, Whom do men say that I the Son of man am? 14 And they said, Some *say that thou art* John the Baptist: some, Elias; and others, Jeremias, or one of the prophets. 15 He saith unto them, But whom say ye that I am? 16 And Simon Peter answered and said, Thou art the Christ, the Son of the living God. 17 And Jesus answered and said unto him, Blessed art thou, Simon Barjona: for flesh and blood hath not revealed *it* unto thee, but my Father which is in heaven. 18 And I say also unto thee, That thou art Peter, and upon this rock {*this confession of faith that Jesus was Jehovah incarnate*} I will build my church; and the gates of hell shall not prevail against it. 19 And I will give unto thee the keys of the kingdom of heaven: and whatsoever thou shalt bind on earth shall be bound in heaven: and whatsoever thou shalt loose on earth shall be loosed in heaven. 20 Then charged he his disciples that they should tell no man that he was Jesus the Christ (Matthew 16:13-20).

The *foundation stone* upon which the whole Church would be built was the public confession of "the Lord Jesus," the incarnate "Son of God." The words "the Lord Jesus" are connected in the one word "Christ" in Peter's confession. It is this confession that opens the door of the New Creation "in Christ" and *causes* the believer to be "born again." This is expressed by the word "for" that begins each verse of Romans 10:10, 11, 12, and 13. The word "for" in each instance is from the Greek word *gar* (gar) meaning *because*. Therefore, each verse begins with the word *because* creating a *continuum of causation* from the first progression to the last, beginning with Romans 10:9.

The first *because* is Romans 10:10 – "For with the heart man believeth unto righteousness; and with the mouth confession is made unto salvation." Notice "confession" is made with "the mouth." Again, this is intended to express Deuteronomy 30:14 – "But the word *is* very nigh unto thee, in thy mouth, and in thy heart, that thou mayest do it." In "confession," "the word" that is "in thy mouth" is released publicly and verbally to express faith in "the Lord Jesus."

The second *because* is found in Romans 10:11 and adds another dimension to confessing Christ – "For the scripture saith, Whosoever believeth on him shall not be ashamed." Here, Paul brings in another Old Testament quote about overcoming the fear of men by confessing Christ. This is a critical point of context considering Christ's statements in Matthew chapter ten and Luke chapter twelve about *confessing Him before men*.

The defining statement about *confessing Christ as Lord* in Romans 10:11 is quoted from Isaiah 28:16. "Therefore thus saith the Lord GOD, Behold, I lay in Zion for a foundation a stone {*the death, burial, and resurrection of Christ*}, a tried stone, a precious corner *stone*, a sure foundation: he that believeth shall not make haste." **The meaning of "shall not make haste" is to flee from pending danger in identifying with Messiah when confessing Him as Jehovah incarnate.** Paul, by inspiration of the Spirit, applies this to *confessing Christ as Lord* and warns about being ashamed of such a confession out of fear, thus denying Christ. This is the context of the warnings in Matthew 10:16-39 and Luke chapter 12:1-12.

> [16] Behold, I send you forth as sheep in the midst of wolves: be ye therefore wise as serpents, and harmless as doves. [17] But beware of men: for they will deliver you up to the

councils, and they will scourge you in their synagogues; [18]
And ye shall be brought before governors and kings for my
sake, for a testimony against them and the Gentiles. [19] But
when they deliver you up, take no thought how or what ye
shall speak: for it shall be given you in that same hour what
ye shall speak. [20] For it is not ye that speak, but the Spirit of
your Father which speaketh in you. [21] And the brother shall
deliver up the brother to death, and the father the child: and
the children shall rise up against *their* parents, and cause
them to be put to death. [22] And ye shall be hated of all *men*
for my name's sake: but he that endureth to the end {*as proof
that his faith is genuine*} shall be saved. [23] But when {*not if*}
they persecute you in this city, flee ye into another: for verily
I say unto you, Ye shall not have gone over the cities of
Israel, till the Son of man be come. [24] The disciple is not
above *his* master, nor the servant above his lord {*Christ died
for us*}. [25] It is enough for the disciple that he be as his
master, and the servant as his lord. If they have called the
master of the house Beelzebub, how much more *shall they
call* them of his household? [26] Fear them not therefore: for
there is nothing covered, that shall not be revealed; and hid,
that shall not be known. [27] What I tell you in darkness, *that*
speak ye in light: and what ye hear in the ear, *that* preach ye
upon the housetops. [28] And fear not them which kill the
body, but are not able to kill the soul: but rather fear him
which is able to destroy both soul and body in hell. [29] Are
not two sparrows sold for a farthing? and one of them shall
not fall on the ground without your Father. [30] But the very
hairs of your head are all numbered. [31] Fear ye not therefore,
ye are of more value than many sparrows. [32] Whosoever
therefore shall confess me before men, him will I confess
also before my Father which is in heaven. [33] But whosoever
shall deny me before men, him will I also deny before my
Father which is in heaven. [34] Think not that I am come to
send peace on earth: I came not to send peace, but a sword.
[35] For I am come to set a man at variance against his father,
and the daughter against her mother, and the daughter in law
against her mother in law. [36] And a man's foes *shall be* they
of his own household. [37] He that loveth father or mother

> more than me is not worthy of me: and he that loveth son or daughter more than me is not worthy of me. [38] And he that taketh not his cross, and followeth after me, is not worthy of me. [39] He that findeth his life shall lose it: and he that loseth his life for my sake shall find it (Matthew 10:16-39).

The statement in Matthew 10:39 is stated a little differently in Luke 9:24. There the phrase is – "For whosoever will save his life shall lose it: but whosoever will lose his life for my sake, the same shall save it." Again, these texts come forth from the context of Isaiah 28:16. "Therefore thus saith the Lord GOD, Behold, I lay in Zion for a foundation a stone {*the death, burial, and resurrection of Christ*}, a tried stone, a precious corner *stone*, a sure foundation: <u>he that believeth shall not make haste</u>." Adam Clarke offers the following comment on Matthew 10:32:

> Whosoever therefore shall confess me before men - That is, whosoever shall acknowledge me to be the Messiah, and have his heart and life regulated by my spirit and doctrine. It is not merely sufficient to have the heart right before God; there must be a firm, manly, and public profession of Christ before men. 'I am no hypocrite,' says one; neither should you be. 'I will keep my religion to myself' i.e. you will not confess Christ before men; then he will renounce you before God.
>
> We confess or own Christ when we own his doctrine, his ministers, his servants, and when no fear hinders us from supporting and assisting them in times of necessity.[3]

John Gill comments on Matthew 10:32 with a similar understanding of the text as Adam Clarke:

> The confession of Christ here, more especially designed, does not so much intend, though it may include, that which is less public, and is necessary to be made by every believer in Christ: for it is not enough to believe in him, with the

[3] Adam Clarke, <u>Adam Clarke's Commentary on the Bible</u> (Nashville: Abingdon Press, 1826) SwordSearcher Software 6.1, (accessed 9/2/2017).

heart, but confession of him must also be made with the mouth; and which lies in ascribing their whole salvation to him, giving him the glory of it; declaring their faith in him to others, and what he has done for their souls; and subjecting themselves to his ordinances, and joining in fellowship with his church and people: which confession, as it ought to be both by words and deeds, and to be hearty and sincere, so likewise visible, open, and before men.[4]

John Gill then offers the following sobering commentary on Matthew 10:33.

will I also deny before my Father which is heaven; he will deny them to be disciples, or that they belong to him; he will deny that he ever knew them, loved or approved of them; he will declare in the presence of his Father, his disapprobation of them, his indignation against them, that they are workers of iniquity; yea, he will do more, he will banish them from his presence, and send them into everlasting burnings.[5]

Christ offers similar warnings in Luke 12:1-12.

1 In the mean time, when there were gathered together an innumerable multitude of people, insomuch that they trode one upon another, he began to say **unto his disciples first of all**, Beware ye of the leaven of the Pharisees, which is
hypocrisy. 2 For there is nothing covered, that shall not be
revealed; neither hid, that shall not be known. 3 Therefore whatsoever ye have spoken in darkness shall be heard in the light; and that which ye have spoken in the ear in closets
shall be proclaimed upon the housetops. 4 And I say unto you my friends, Be not afraid of them that kill the body, and after
that have no more that they can do. 5 **But I will forewarn you whom ye shall fear: Fear him, which after he hath killed hath power to cast into hell; yea, I say unto you,**

---

[4] John Gill, John Gill's Exposition of the Entire Bible (London: Matthews & Leigh, 1810), SwordSearcher Software 6.1 (accessed 9/2/2017).
[5] Ibid.

Fear him. [6] Are not five sparrows sold for two farthings, and not one of them is forgotten before God? [7] But even the very hairs of your head are all numbered. **Fear not therefore**: ye are of more value than many sparrows. [8] Also I say unto you, **Whosoever shall confess me before men, him shall the Son of man also confess before the angels of God: [9] But he that denieth me before men shall be denied before the angels of God**. [10] And whosoever shall speak a word against the Son of man, it shall be forgiven him: but unto him that blasphemeth against the Holy Ghost it shall not be forgiven {*this is the rejection and hatred of that which the Spirit of God convicts about the Person of Jesus; therefore unbelief*}. [11] And when they bring you unto the synagogues, and *unto* magistrates, and powers, take ye no thought how or what thing ye shall answer, or what ye shall say: [12] For the Holy Ghost shall teach you in the same hour what ye ought to say (Luke 12:1-12).

[21] Not every one that saith unto me, Lord, Lord, shall enter into the kingdom of heaven; but he that doeth the will of my Father which is in heaven. [22] Many will say to me in that day, Lord, Lord, have we not prophesied in thy name? and in thy name have cast out devils? and in thy name done many wonderful works? [23] And then will I profess unto them, I never knew you: depart from me, ye that work iniquity (Matthew 7:21-23).

[1] Beloved, believe not every spirit, but try the spirits whether they are of God: because many false prophets are gone out into the world. [2] Hereby know ye the Spirit of God: **Every spirit that confesseth that Jesus Christ is come in the flesh is of God: [3] And every spirit that confesseth not that Jesus Christ is come in the flesh is not of God: and this is that *spirit* of antichrist**, whereof ye have heard that it should come; and even now already is it in the world (I John 4:1-3).

Questions for Discussion

1. Discuss why it is important to understand that the context of Romans 10:1-13 is particularly written to Jews to correct the corruption of the Gospel that added the conditions of the Mosaic Covenant as necessities for salvation.

2. Discuss the meaning of the word "end" in Romans 10:4 and the significance of the fact that the Law *aimed* at something it could never achieve.

3. Discuss Romans 10:5-7 from the context of Leviticus 18:5 from which these verses come. Especially discuss the fact that the Law was given for *relational purposes*, not *salvational purposes*.

4. The KJV translators have ended Romans 10:8 with a semicolon to show us the connection between two transitional phrases that are closely related. In other words, "the word of faith, which we preach" is going to be defined in Romans 10:9. Discuss the significance of this statement to understanding and defining a biblical *faith response* to the Gospel in the three verbs that follow in Romans 10:9-13.

5. Discuss why the "word" of faith that was "in thy mouth" per Deuteronomy 30:14 must be *verbally expressed* as compared to what Peter testified/witnessed/confessed in Matthew 16:13-20.

Chapter Seven

Calling Jesus Lord

Matthew chapters five through seven and Luke chapter six give us the message of Christ that defines what it means to be a *Christian*. We can be confident that this message was preached by Jesus on numerous occasions as He traveled throughout Israel preaching and teaching. This message defines the expectations of the New Covenant and how Jesus expected His disciples to live their lives after they were "born again" of the Spirit of God. None of the statements in Luke 6:37-46 are conditions for salvation. The statements define a lifestyle for those already saved. According to Luke 6:40, the text is clearly addressed to those claiming to be "disciples," or followers of the teachings of Jesus.

> 37 Judge not, and ye shall not be judged: condemn not, and ye shall not be condemned: forgive, and ye shall be forgiven: 38 Give, and it shall be given unto you; good measure, pressed down, and shaken together, and running over, shall men give into your bosom. For with the same measure that ye mete withal it shall be measured to you again. 39 And he spake a parable unto them, Can the blind lead the blind? shall they not both fall into the ditch? 40 **The disciple** is not above his master: but every one that is perfect {*complete or spiritually mature*} shall be as his master. 41 And why beholdest thou the mote that is in thy brother's eye, but perceivest not the beam that is in thine own eye? 42 Either how canst thou say to thy brother, Brother, let me pull out the mote that is in thine eye, when thou thyself beholdest not the beam that is in thine own eye? Thou hypocrite, cast out first the beam out of thine own eye {*take care of your own corruptions first because duplicity will corrupt all your ministry attempts*}, **and then** shalt thou see clearly to pull out the mote that is in thy brother's eye. 43 For a good tree bringeth not forth corrupt fruit; neither doth a corrupt tree bring forth good fruit. 44 For every tree is known by his own fruit. For of thorns men do not gather figs, nor of a bramble

bush gather they grapes. [45] A good man out of the good treasure of his heart bringeth forth that which is good; and an evil man out of the evil treasure of his heart bringeth forth that which is evil: for of the abundance of the heart his mouth speaketh. [46] And **why call ye me, Lord, Lord, and do not the things which I say** (Luke 6:37-46)?

The ultimate test for anyone's hypocrisy is to answer a simple question. "Why call ye me, Lord, Lord, and do not the things which I say" (Luke 6:45)? The responsibilities that accompany confessing Jesus to be Lord (Jehovah incarnate in human form) are significant. God has very high expectations for the way His "born again" children live their lives before Him and before the world. Every "born again" child of God is responsible to represent the character and nature of God to the world. Matthew chapters five through seven and Luke chapter six define exactly how believers are to represent God to the world. This representation defines the priesthood of all New Covenant believers. God expects the lives of His priests to excel in the ways defined by Luke 6:37-46. Failure in these areas was the failure of the Levitical priesthood of the Mosaic Covenant and the reason God removed them from service. This removal is the substance of most of the book of Malachi.

[6] A son honoureth *his* father, and a servant his master: if then I *be* a father, where *is* mine honour? and if I *be* a master, where *is* my fear? saith the LORD of hosts unto you, O priests, that despise my name. And ye say, **Wherein have we despised thy name?** [7] Ye offer polluted bread upon mine altar; and ye say, Wherein have we polluted thee? In that ye say, The table of the LORD *is* contemptible. [8] And if ye offer the blind for sacrifice, *is it* not evil? and if ye offer the lame and sick, *is it* not evil? offer it now unto thy governor; will he be pleased with thee, or accept thy person? saith the LORD of hosts. [9] And now, I pray you, beseech God that he will be gracious unto us: this hath been by your means: will he regard your persons? saith the LORD of hosts. [10] Who *is there* even among you that would shut the doors *for nought*? neither do ye kindle *fire* on mine altar for nought. I have no

> pleasure in you, saith the LORD of hosts, neither will I accept an offering at your hand. [11] For from the rising of the sun even unto the going down of the same my name *shall be* great among the Gentiles; and in every place incense *shall be* offered unto my name, and a pure offering: for my name *shall be* great among the heathen, saith the LORD of hosts. [12] But ye have profaned it, in that ye say, The table of the LORD *is* polluted; and the fruit thereof, *even* his meat, *is* contemptible. [13] Ye said also, Behold, what a weariness *is it*! and ye have snuffed at it, saith the LORD of hosts; and ye brought *that which was* torn, and the lame, and the sick; thus ye brought an offering: should I accept this of your hand? saith the LORD. [14] But cursed *be* the deceiver, which hath in his flock a male, and voweth, and sacrificeth unto the Lord a corrupt thing: for I *am* a great King, saith the LORD of hosts, and my name *is* dreadful {*reverential fear*} among the heathen (Malachi 1:6-14).

This is the sobering context of the warnings of Jesus to professing disciples in Luke 6:47-49 and Matthew 7:21-27. The context of the warning to professing disciples (professed followers of the commands and teachings of Jesus) is the subtlety of self-deception about the reality of genuine faith/belief in God. Clearly, the practices of Malachi 1:6-14 reveal religious practices that do not reflect a belief that the God to which those worship practices were directed cared about the way they lived their lives. The pitiful nature of offering the sick, blind, and lame animals for sacrifice reflected a very low worth put upon God.

However, more significant to the warning of Jesus is the fact that such "works" reflected unbelief on the part of those offering such sacrifices. Why else would someone offer such pitiful excuses for worship to the "Lord of lords and King of kings"? Would someone dare bring such pitiful excuses for an offering to any earthly king? Certainly, not! The earthy king would immediately be offended and have such a person punished, if not killed for such a disgraceful and disrespectful offering. Why then would someone think he could escape God's judgment for such wickedness? This reveals a false faith and a false profession.

This is to where Jesus leads such a person in Luke 6:47-49 and Matthew 7:21-27.

> [47] Whosoever cometh to me, and heareth my sayings, and doeth them, I will shew you **to whom he is like**: [48] He is like a man which built an house, and digged deep, and laid the foundation on a rock: and when the flood arose, the stream beat vehemently upon that house, and could not shake it: for it was founded upon a rock. [49] But he that heareth, and doeth not, is like a man that without a foundation built an house upon the earth; against which the stream did beat vehemently, and immediately it fell; and the ruin of that house was great (Luke 6:47-49).

This warning is much greater than merely warning about wasting one's life on riotous living and worldly philosophies. The warning is given to those that profess to be "born again" followers of Jesus Christ, but who do not give due diligence to doing what Jesus said to do. This is not speaking of some type of *sinless perfection* where a person always does exactly what Jesus taught. We are all pieces of clay with great weaknesses and cracks. Jesus wants to see genuine effort, honesty, and transparency as we seek to live the way Jesus taught us to live. However, when our effort, honesty, and transparency is intended only to deceive other human onlookers while thinking we are something we are not, this is the worst kind of self-deception. This kind of self-deception will take people to the fires and torments of Hell. We must never forget that genuinely being part of the Gospel of the Kingdom involves believing and being in subjection to the *all-knowing* and *all-seeing* King of the Kingdom.

> [21] **Not every one that saith unto me, Lord, Lord, shall enter into the kingdom of heaven; but he that doeth the will of my Father which is in heaven**. [22] Many will say to me in that day, Lord, Lord, have we not prophesied in thy name? and in thy name have cast out devils? and in thy name done many wonderful works? [23] And then will I profess unto them, I never knew you: depart from me, ye that work iniquity. [24] **Therefore** whosoever heareth these sayings of

> mine, and doeth them, I will liken him unto a wise man, which built his house upon a rock: [25] And the rain descended, and the floods came, and the winds blew, and beat upon that house; and it fell not: for it was founded upon a rock. [26] And every one that heareth these sayings of mine, and doeth them not, shall be likened unto a foolish man, which built his house upon the sand: [27] And the rain descended, and the floods came, and the winds blew, and beat upon that house; and it fell: and great was the fall of it (Matthew 7:21-27).

The double declaration "Lord, Lord" is the public declaration of a subject/servant regarding the sovereign authority and protection of his declared King/Lord. The *rights* of citizenship are accompanied with the *obligations* of citizenship to live in obedience to the dictates and commands of the Sovereign. To declare one's self a subject of the King without living in subjection to the King is a contradiction to such declarations. Even more so, when one willfully makes such a declaration with no real desire to be in obedient subjection, such a contradiction could be viewed as treasonous. This latter scenario seems to be the substance of the warning of Jesus in Matthew 7:21-27. The important difference between the warning in Luke chapter six and the warning in Matthew chapter seven is that Jesus connects such disobedience to a false profession of faith. This is the important transition between Ephesians 2:1-3 into 2:4-9 into the statement of Ephesians 2:10. If we truly believe that Jesus Christ is the incarnate, omniscient, omnipresent Sovereign Lord, this reality will radically change the way we live our lives before His eyes.

It is critical to see the *transition of expectations* from Ephesians 2:1-3 into the next few verses in Ephesians 2:4-10. The word "but" in Ephesians 2:4 begins a *juxtaposition* (placing these two contrasting statements side-by-side for comparison). All Church Age believer/priests have many new privileges and responsibilities that are often taken for granted. This is especially true of Gentile believers who are ignorant of the obligations of the ceremonial and sacrificial aspects of the Mosaic Covenant (the Law). The contrasts between Ephesians 2:1-3 and Ephesians 2:4-10 are radical.

> 1 And you *hath he quickened*, who were dead in trespasses and sins; 2 Wherein in time past ye walked according to the course of this world, according to the prince of the power of the air, the spirit that now worketh in the children of disobedience: 3 Among whom also we all had our conversation {*practice/manner of living*} in times past in the lusts of our flesh, fulfilling the desires of the flesh and of the mind; and were by nature the children of wrath, even as others (Ephesians 2:1-3).

1. We were "dead in trespasses and sins."
2. In the past, "ye walked according to the course of this world."
3. Ye were once led by "the prince of the power of the air" (Satan).
4. Our lifestyles were exceedingly corrupted by yielding to "the lusts of our flesh."
5. We were "the children of wrath."

As we read Ephesians 2:4-10, we see the extreme contrast in the believers' new position "in Christ Jesus" defining extreme new expectations of all believers. By my count, Paul uses this phrase "in Christ Jesus" at least forty times in his epistles, six times in the first three chapters of Ephesians alone. The phrase is theologically significant as it reveals the believer's security in his new eternal position in "the regeneration" (Matthew 19:28).

> 4 But God, who is rich in mercy, for his great love wherewith he loved us, 5 Even when we were dead in sins, hath quickened us **together** with Christ, (by grace ye are saved {*perfect, passive, participle*};) 6 And hath raised *us* up **together**, and made *us* sit **together** in heavenly *places* in Christ Jesus: 7 That in the ages to come he might shew the exceeding riches of his grace in *his* kindness toward us through Christ Jesus. 8 For by grace {*God's provision*} are {*present tense*} ye saved {*perfect, passive, participle*} through faith {*man's response*}; and that not of yourselves: {*salvation*} *it is* the gift of God: 9 Not of works, lest any man should boast. 10 For we are his workmanship, created {*aorist, passive, participle*} in Christ Jesus unto good works, which

God hath before ordained that we should walk in them (Ephesians 2:4-10).

This *juxtaposition* begins with the answer to man's dilemma – "but God." Into this horrible and devastating spiritual darkness of humanity's fallen state bursts forth the wondrous light of the mercy of God's grace. All of humanity is hopelessly lost in the condemnation by the righteousness of God. It is an overwhelming and supernatural problem that requires an overwhelming and supernatural solution. No person can save himself. He is "condemned already" (John 3:18). No one can work himself out of the depth of his fallen and condemned state. There is no ritual that can cleanse him of the filth of his sin. There is but one hope – the grace and mercy of God.

We would think we would find mankind's history riddle with accounts of men pleading with God to be saved. Instead, we find God pleading with man to receive His gift of salvation. This is true because we are blind to our condition before God. We are blind to the holiness of God and the perfect righteousness of God. Only God truly understands the totality and depth of our fall into sin and condemnation. Only God understands what is necessary to our rescue from that fallen state. God requires a supernatural solution. Only God can supernaturally provide that solution. Men foolishly think that they can somehow earn God's favor and pardon. Men foolishly think that some ritual or sacrifice can take away our sin and cleanse us before God. That is what apostate Israel had come to believe by the time of the prophet Isaiah and just before their captivity. God has always had but *one way* to reconciliation with Him – "by grace through faith." The *one way* to reconciliation has NEVER been through religion! This is, and always has been, Satan's great corruption of "the faith."

[10] Hear the word of the LORD, ye rulers of Sodom; give ear unto the law of our God, ye people of Gomorrah. [11] To what purpose *is* the multitude of your sacrifices unto me? saith the LORD: I am full of the burnt offerings of rams, and the fat of fed beasts; and I delight not in the blood of bullocks, or of lambs, or of he goats. [12] When ye come to appear before me, who hath required this at your hand, to tread my courts? [13]

> Bring no more vain oblations; incense is an abomination unto me; the new moons and sabbaths, the calling of assemblies, I cannot away with; *it is* iniquity, even the solemn meeting. 14 Your new moons and your appointed feasts my soul hateth: they are a trouble unto me; I am weary to bear *them.* 15 And when ye spread forth your hands, I will hide mine eyes from you: yea, when ye make many prayers, I will not hear: your hands are full of blood. 16 Wash you, make you clean; put away the evil of your doings from before mine eyes; cease to do evil; 17 Learn to do well; seek judgment, relieve the oppressed, judge the fatherless, plead for the widow. 18 Come now, and let us reason together, saith the LORD: though your sins be as scarlet, they shall be as white as snow; though they be red like crimson, they shall be as wool. 19 If ye be willing and obedient, ye shall eat the good of the land: 20 But if ye refuse and rebel, ye shall be devoured with the sword: for the mouth of the LORD hath spoken *it* (Isaiah 1:10-20).

The sacrifices and holy days of the Mosaic Covenant were given to be reminders to Israel of the means that gifted them their promised redemption. The thrust of God's rebuke of the children of Israel was that they had gradually made the sacrifices and holy days merely *mechanical*. They participated in their continual worship rituals without any real thought of Who God is, what those rituals meant, or any real worship being offered to God. **Worship is the primary offering of everything a believer does**. Worship declares our view of God's worth in our redemption and our daily life in fellowship with Him. The rituals of worship soon replaced true worship. God hates this nonsense.

This is what always happens when doctrine is corrupted. When doctrine is corrupted, people proportionately begin to become the focus of worship rather than God. True doctrine is always God-centered (Theocentric). The focus is always upon the worth of God in our lives. False doctrines corrupt worship making it man-centered (anthropocentric). It is not that man is actually worshiped. It is that man's needs and wants become the focus of worship.

True worship is right doctrine that leads men to the throne of grace to humble themselves at the feet of God. True worship exposes man for what he is in the eyes of God. True worship brings that sinner to see and understand all that God is and then offers that sinner God's benevolent provisions of His grace. Then, that sinner enters true worship being offered to God. To receive what God's benevolent grace offers without returning worship to God is to completely corrupt worship. This was the corruption of the Mosaic Covenant by the priesthood that God addresses in Isaiah 1:10-20.

Isaiah 1:10-20 has similarities to the statement in Ephesians 2:1-10. The ultimate point of the difference between Ephesians 2:1-3 and 2:4-10 is that God's intent in *everyone's* life ("whosoever") is to restore them to full fellowship with Him. This begins by offering the free gift of salvation to all "by grace through faith" and continues in their progressive sanctification "by grace through faith." In other words, God is *universally benevolent* ("the world," John 3:16). Salvation just opens the door of opportunity for that fellowship. God *wants* to bless people. God *wants* to walk with us and talk with us. God *wants* us to pray and He *wants* to answer our prayers. If we will repent of sin and "dead works," understand and believe the Gospel, confess Jesus to be Jehovah incarnate, and call on the Name of Jesus to save us from Hell, God will indwell us in the Person of the Holy Spirit. He will then **begin** a supernatural work of progressive transfiguration in our lives from within. We are literally God's "workmanship, created in Christ Jesus unto good works." Wow! If you cannot find something for which to praise God and to worship Him in that truth, you probably better reinvestigate the reality of your understanding of what God has done for you. God deserves to be worshiped. Worship should be the preoccupation of every moment of the life of a believer.

God is "rich in mercy, for his great love wherewith he loved us" Ephesians 2:4. What a remarkable statement. Consider the infinite depth of these few words. See if you can find a place where the riches of God's mercy and love do not touch your life. You will never discover such a place, because God loves us "**even when we were dead in sins**" (Ephesians 2:5). God loves you "**even when**."

When we correctly understand the infinite depth and breadth of God's love, then right doctrine will also generate loving obedience. Learning Scripture to know, and then do, God's will become a priority in those that want to truly worship God "in Spirit and in truth" (John 4:24). Salvation is intended to do much more than merely give us a fire escape from Hell. Salvation is intended to open a door to fellowship with God that is immersed in our adoration, praise, and worship of God. Every aspect of Bible study answers the question, is God worthy of worship? If every aspect of your Bible study does not arrive at that conclusion, your understanding is corrupted. That is the intent of the emphasis on the word "truth" in Christ's teaching in John 4:24. None can truly worship God until he truly understands his condemnation, the Gospel, and the overwhelming wonders of the gift of salvation. God's love reached into the cesspool of humanity to rescue sinners drowning in the filth of their own degradation. We will never grasp that analogy until we grasp God's holiness and purity along with His hatred of impurity.

People just cannot seem to grasp the concept of what it means to take up our cross and follow Him. The point is that the Cross of Christ fills our lives. We must let go of everything else before we can take up that Cross. It is a complete/total commitment that empties our lives of everything worldly and then fills our lives with everything that is important.

"Even when we were dead in sins" (Ephesians 2:5a) - most people view sin as a mere sickness or a deadly disease. This view of sin is completely corrupt. When sin entered humanity through Adam, it did not make Adam sick. Sin slayed Adam. The words "dead in sins" portray a vivid word picture. The word "dead" is from the Greek word *nekros* (nek-ros'). The root word for this is *nekus*, which refers to *a corpse*. Therefore, the word picture is that of a *dead corpse*. In Ephesians 2:1, God tells us we were dead in trespasses and sins. Then, He repeats Himself and tells us we were "dead in sins." Both the words "trespasses" and "sins" are in the *locative case*. That is why we have the word "in." The words "trespasses" and "sins" describe the *location* of this dead corpse. **The word picture is more than a dead corpse in a grave. The word picture is that of a dead corpse buried in a death of eternal separation from God in a place called Hell.** The grace of God in the gift of salvation and eternal life removes the believing sinner out of the *location* of being "dead in trespasses and sins." How can we understand all of this and call Jesus "Lord, Lord" and not do the things He says to do?

> [11] For the grace of God that bringeth salvation hath appeared to all men, [12] **Teaching us that**, **denying ungodliness and worldly lusts, we should live soberly, righteously, and godly, in this present world**; [13] Looking for that blessed hope, and the glorious appearing of the great God and our Saviour Jesus Christ; [14] Who gave himself for us, that he might redeem us from all iniquity, **and** purify unto himself a peculiar people, zealous of good works. [15] These things speak, and exhort, and rebuke with all authority. Let no man despise thee (Titus 2:11-15).

Questions for Discussion

1. Discuss how Matthew chapters five through seven and Luke chapter six define what it means to call Jesus your Lord.

2. Thoroughly discuss Jesus' following question defining His expectations of the confessor in what it means to call Him Lord. "And why call ye me, Lord, Lord, and do not the things which I say" (Luke 6:37-46)?

3. Malachi 1:6-14 is a warning to the Levitical priesthood of Israel about the hypocritical manifestations of confessing faith in God while living and practicing their priesthood in hypocritical contradiction to that confession. Discuss how this context is important to Romans 10:9-13.

4. From the context of the warnings given by Jesus in Luke 6:47-49 and Matthew 7:21-27, discuss how these warnings deal with the hypocrisy of the individual that calls Jesus Lord and then does not do what Jesus commands.

5. Discuss the contrasts between Ephesians 2:1-3 and Ephesians 2:4-10 and God's expectations of those that truly understand what it means to call Jesus Lord.

Chapter Eight

Calling on the Name of Jesus

Having carefully and inductively examined the Scriptures up to this point to ensure that we understand the verbs (action words) that define saving faith, we come to the fourth verb in the order of these verbs – "call on the Name of the Lord" (Romans 10:13). The event of salvation never will take place if this fourth verb is not completed. Therefore, O*nly Believism* is such a dangerous corruption of a biblical response to the Gospel. Repenting of sin and "dead works," understanding and believing the Gospel, and confessing Jesus as Lord do not save us until we call on Jesus to save us.

Paul is addressing the corruption of the Mosaic Covenant by the priesthood of Israel in Romans chapter ten. The priesthood had corrupted the Mosaic Covenant by applying its purpose to individual righteousness and salvation rather than national righteousness. The "blessing and a curse" of the Mosaic Covenant was conditioned upon the *national* righteousness of Israel. It was never intended for *individual* salvation. This is clearly detailed in Deuteronomy 11:1-32. This is a lengthy text, but warrants our carefully examination to establish the context of Romans chapter ten.

> [1] Therefore thou shalt love the LORD thy God, and {*as an expression of loving the LORD*} keep {*observe, preserve, and/or reserve*} his charge {*custody with the idea of preservation*}, and his statutes {*ordinance or legal, governing, decree of Law*}, and his judgments {*various judicially decreed sentences for breaking God's individual ordinances*}, and his commandments {*used collectively of the Law as a whole*}, always {*from one sunset to the next; i.e., continuously*}
> [2] And know ye {*plural, therefore collectively*} this day {*The intent of the following warning is that the future generations will not know the wondrous works of God in delivering Israel apart from the present generation educating them and keeping/preserving these*

truths throughout their generations.}: for *I speak* not with your children which have not known, and which have not seen the chastisement of the LORD your God, his greatness, his mighty hand, and his stretched out arm, [3] And his miracles, and his acts, which he did in the midst of Egypt unto Pharaoh the king of Egypt, and unto all his land; [4] And what he did unto the army of Egypt, unto their horses, and to their chariots; how he made the water of the Red sea to overflow them as they pursued after you, and *how* the LORD hath destroyed them unto this day; [5] And what he did unto you in the wilderness, until ye came into this place; [6] And what he did unto Dathan and Abiram, the sons of Eliab, the son of Reuben: how the earth opened her mouth, and swallowed them up, and their households, and their tents, and all the substance that *was* in their possession, in the midst of all Israel: [7] But your eyes have seen all the great acts of the LORD which he did {*Only the males over the age of twenty years living at the time of the failure in faith at Kadesh-Barnea were cursed to die in the Wilderness. "No males under twenty years of age, no females, and none of the tribe of Levi, were objects of the denunciation."*[6]} [8] Therefore shall ye keep all the commandments which I command you this day, **that ye may be strong, and go in and possess the land, whither ye go to possess it**; [9] And that ye may prolong *your* {*collectively referring to the nation of Israel*} days in the land, which the LORD sware unto your fathers to give unto them and to their seed, a land that floweth with milk and honey. [10] For the land, whither thou goest in to possess it, *is* not as the land of Egypt, from whence ye came out, where thou sowedst thy seed, and wateredst *it* with thy foot, as a garden of herbs: [11] But the land, whither ye go to possess it, *is* a land of hills and valleys, *and* drinketh water of the rain of heaven: [12] A land which the LORD thy God careth for: the eyes of the LORD thy God *are* always upon it, from the beginning of the year even unto

[6] Robert Jamieson, A.R. Fausset, and David Brown, Jamieson-Fausset-Brown Commentary (Peabody: Hendrickson Publishers, 1996), SwordSearcher Software 6.1 (accessed 9/2/2017).

the end of the year. 13 And it shall come to pass, **if** {*conditioned upon doing what verse 1 says*} ye {*national Israel*} shall hearken diligently unto my commandments {*the whole Law corporately*} which I command you this day, **to love the LORD your God, and to serve him with all your heart and with all your soul**, 14 That I will give *you* {*the blessing of*} the rain of your land in his due season, the first rain and the latter rain, that thou mayest gather in thy corn, and thy wine, and thine oil. 15 And I will send grass in thy fields for thy cattle, that thou mayest eat and be full. 16 **Take heed to yourselves, that your heart be not deceived, and ye turn aside**, and serve other gods, and worship them; 17 And *then* the LORD'S wrath {*the curse*} be kindled against you {*national Israel*}, and he shut up the heaven, that there be no rain, and that the land yield not her fruit; and *lest* ye perish quickly from off the good land which the LORD giveth you. 18 **Therefore shall ye lay up these my words** {*the blessing and curse instructions regarding the Mosaic Covenant as a beloved treasure*} in your heart and in your soul, and bind them for a sign upon your hand, that they may be as frontlets between your eyes. 19 And ye shall teach them your children {*putting upon the parents and nation the responsibility of the preservation to future generations*}, speaking of them when thou sittest in thine house, and when thou walkest by the way, when thou liest down, and when thou risest up. 20 And thou shalt write them upon the door posts of thine house, and upon thy gates: 21 That your days may be multiplied {*collectively referring to the nation of Israel*}, and the days of your children, in the land which the LORD sware unto your fathers to give them, as the days of heaven upon the earth. 22 For if ye shall diligently keep all these commandments which I command you, **to do them, to love the LORD your God, to walk in all his ways, and to cleave unto him**; 23 Then {*conditional blessing*} will the LORD drive out all these nations from before you, and ye {*collectively referring to the nation of Israel*} shall possess greater nations and mightier than yourselves. 24 Every place whereon the soles of your feet shall tread shall be yours: from the wilderness and Lebanon,

> from the river, the river Euphrates, even unto the uttermost sea shall your coast be. 25 There shall no man be able to stand before you: *for* the LORD your God shall lay the fear of you and the dread of you upon all the land that ye shall tread upon, as he hath said unto you. 26 **Behold, I set before you this day a blessing and a curse**; 27 **A blessing, if ye obey** the commandments of the LORD your God, which I command you this day: 28 And **a curse, if ye will not obey** the commandments of the LORD your God, but turn aside out of the way which I command you this day, to go after other gods, which ye have not known. 29 And **it shall come to pass**, when the LORD thy God hath brought thee in unto the land whither thou goest to possess it, that thou shalt put the blessing upon mount Gerizim {*fruitfulness*}, and the curse upon mount Ebal {*barrenness*}. 30 *Are* they not on the other side Jordan, by the way where the sun goeth down, in the land of the Canaanites, which dwell in the champaign over against Gilgal, beside the plains of Moreh? 31 For ye shall pass over Jordan to go in to possess the land which the LORD your God giveth you, and ye shall possess it, and dwell therein. 32 And **ye shall observe to do all the statutes and judgments which I set before you this day** (Deuteronomy 11:1-32).

We can clearly see that the "righteousness which is of the law" (Romans 10:5) referred to the *national* righteousness of national Israel as they fulfilled the conditions of the Mosaic Covenant. The Mosaic Covenant (the Law) was never intended to be an avenue for individual salvific righteousness. The God-kind righteousness of salvific justification could never be achieved by any means. Nor was Law-keeping ever intended to be a means for justification; i.e. the imputation or impartation (depending upon the point in history before or after the Day of Pentecost) of God-kind righteousness to the believing sinner.

If individuals within the nation of Israel broke the Law, the *leaders* of national Israel were required to administrate justice per the "judgments" for various failures as detailed within the Law. If the leadership of Israel failed to administrate justice, God's "curse" would come against the nation of Israel instead of the individual.

If the leadership of Israel faithfully administrated the "judgments" of the Law, God's blessings would remain upon the nation of Israel. This is the context of God's promise to Solomon in II Chronicles 7:14 after the prayer of dedication of the new Temple in Jerusalem.

> [12] And the LORD appeared to Solomon by night, and said unto him, I have heard thy prayer, and have chosen this place to myself for an house of sacrifice. [13] **If I** shut up heaven that there be no rain, or **if I** command the locusts to devour the land, or **if I** send pestilence among my people; [14] **If my people**, which are called by my name, shall humble themselves, and pray, and seek my face, and turn from their wicked ways; then will I hear from heaven, and will forgive their sin, and will heal their land (II Chronicles 7:12-14).

Clearly, individual salvation of every Jew in the nation of Israel was not part of God's *blessing promise,* should the leadership of Israel administrate justice as defined by the Mosaic Covenant (the Law). That was never God's intent in giving the Law to national Israel. Nevertheless, this is what most of Israel's leadership had come to believe and had been teaching the Jewish people for centuries. Therefore, the clear majority of the Jews had "[2b] a zeal of God, but not according to knowledge. [3] For they being ignorant of God's righteousness, and going about to establish their own righteousness, have not submitted themselves unto the righteousness of God" (Rom 10:2b-3). This is the context with which we begin Romans chapter ten.

There is little doubt that Romans chapter ten is directed to Jews within national Israel. Romans is directed to Jews who had been misled by the Old Covenant priesthood into misplacing their faith in keeping the Mosaic Covenant (Moralism and Ritualism) *to be saved.* Because the objective facts of their faith were misplaced, the actions of their faith and the purpose for those actions were wrong and heretical. Although they had both "zeal for God" and faith in God, both their zeal and their faith were based on their ignorance of God-kind righteousness necessary to salvation. Therefore, they remained lost because of misplace faith.

It was not enough to merely believe *in* God. They

needed to believe the correct things about God, about themselves, and they needed to understand what God had done to deliver them from the condemnation of sin before they could respond to the Gospel according to God's directions. We can find a *straight-line pattern* of this in Romans 10:1-13 to God's expected responses to an understanding of the details of the Gospel of Jesus Christ.

1. They needed to **understand** their ignorance of God's righteousness (God-kind righteousness) and **understand** that they could never attain or achieve that kind of righteousness through Moralism or Ritualism. Then, they needed to **repent** of their "dead works" (Hebrews 6:1) and the sin of self-righteousness (Romans 10:1-7).
2. They needed to **understand** that salvation could not come through any form of human accomplishment, but only "by grace through **faith**" in the sinless life, the *finished* substitutionary Cross-work of the death of Jesus Christ, His burial, and His resurrection/glorification (Romans 10:8).
3. They needed to **act** upon those **understood** and **believed** details of the Gospel of Jesus Christ by:

A. Confessing Jesus to be Jehovah (Romans 10:9-10)
B. Believing with their hearts every detail of the Gospel and resting their eternal souls in the Person of Jesus and His preserving care (Romans 10:9-10)
C. Believing the Gospel and **confessing** Jesus to be Jehovah
D. Call -the sinner is **then**, and only **then**, directed to **call** on the Name of Jesus to save him (Romans 10:13)

Obviously, Romans 10:1-13 is dealing with salvation, defining and detailing a biblical response to the Gospel of Jesus Christ ("believe") and a biblical response to the Person of Jesus Christ ("confess . . .as LORD"). Yet, there is still a fundamental perpetuation of ignorance today within most of professing *Christianity.* This ignorance is about the difference between the kind of righteousness that comes by man's *doing* (man-kind righteousness) and God's *doing.* The righteousness that comes "by grace through faith" (God-kind righteousness) is God's *doing* (through the death, burial, and resurrection of Jesus Christ).

And it shall come to pass that whosoever shall **call on the name of the LORD** {*Jehovah*} shall be delivered (Joel 2:32a).

> [11] For the scripture saith, Whosoever believeth on him shall not be ashamed. [12] For there is no difference between the Jew and the Greek; for the same Lord over all is rich unto all that call upon him. [13] For **whosoever shall call upon the name of the Lord shall be saved** (Romans 10:11-13).

The words *receive* and *confess* are very much interrelated. They are not equal to *believing* as the *Soteriological Reductionists* would have us believe. Neither is *receiving* Christ equal to *confessing* Christ as LORD. The important truth about *receiving* and *confessing* is Who we are *receiving* and *confessing.* Understanding the Person Whom we are *receiving* and *confessing* gives considerable depth to what we are doing as these two terms interrelate with believing. This understanding then connects us deeply, intimately, and intricately to the spiritual convictions that turn our hearts from sin to "repentance toward God, and faith toward our Lord Jesus Christ" (Acts 20:21). This understanding must precede *confessin*g and *receiving* Jesus as LORD.

As we have seen from, each of these individual verb responses to the Gospel message are individual and different responses. Yet, they are very much interrelated. If one's faith response truly exists, it must lead us to the next response in a specific order.

Believing that Jesus is a holy, righteous, and just God and that we are sinners before Him, necessitates that we will respond in humility before Him in repentance. If repentance is not the response of this understanding, we do not really understand Who Jesus is or the consequences of our sinfulness before Him. He is the just Judge and we are already condemned and guilty sinners before Him (John 3:18).

> [16] For God so loved the world, that he gave his only begotten Son, that whosoever believeth in him should not perish, but have everlasting life. [17] For God sent not his Son into the world to condemn the world; but that the world through him

> might be saved. [18] He that believeth on him is not condemned: **but he that believeth not is condemned already**, because he hath not believed in the name of the only begotten Son of God. [19] And this is the condemnation, that light is come into the world, and men loved darkness rather than light, because their deeds were evil. [20] For every one that doeth evil hateth the light, neither cometh to the light, lest his deeds should be reproved. [21] But he that doeth truth cometh to the light, that his deeds may be made manifest, that they are wrought in God (John 3:16-20).

It is important that we connect each of these terms (repent, receive, believe, and confess) to the next interrelated word, which is *call*. As already established, Romans 10:13 is a quote from Joel 2:32. Although the truth and application is relevant to all sinners (the intent of the word "whosever"), Paul's instruction in Romans 10:13 is directed primarily in this text to *national* Israel (Romans 10:1) of which the clear majority of individuals needed to be saved in order to become part of true Israel (spiritual/saved Israel). Our understanding of Romans 10:13 must come from our understanding of Joel 2:32. Our understanding of these two texts cannot be *contradictory*. Our understanding of these two texts must be *complimentary*.

The word "call" from Joel 2:32 is translated from the Hebrew word *qara'* (kaw-raw'). Although the primary meaning of the word simply means *to address someone by their name*, the context of Joel 2:32 gives us a much deeper meaning by the implication of the circumstances that surround the instruction. The context of Joel chapter two is the restoration of national Israel from God's national judgment due to national Israel's failure to keep the conditions of the Mosaic Covenant.

As we have already seen from Deuteronomy 11:1-32, the Mosaic Covenant was a "blessing and a curse" covenant for *national* Israel. Because the leadership of *national* Israel failed to enforce the requirements of the Mosaic Covenant, God judged *national Israel* with the *Times of the Gentiles* (the seventy weeks of years or seventy *Heptads* of Daniel 9:24). Sixty-nine of those weeks have already been fulfilled in history. The seventieth week of years (a *Heptad*) is the Seven Year Tribulation of God's promised judgment of the nations. After this seventieth week, God will restore national Israel to world dominion under the Lordship of Jesus Christ.

God's judgment upon national Israel during the *Times of the Gentiles* has taken the form of various captivities and persecutions. Although individual Jews could repent, believe, and be saved at any time during the *Times of the Gentiles*, God required national repentance for the restoration of national Israel. This national repentance will take place during the Seven Year Tribulation in God's judgment of the nations.

There were numerous movements that sought to lead the nation of Israel into repentance down through the years of the *Times of the Gentiles*. The last movement was at the time of Jesus Christ from a group known as the *Baptists* (Sons of Righteousness). At the time of Christ, the spokesman for this group was a prophet and preacher named John *the Baptist*. We cannot separate John *the Baptist's* ministry from the message of God's continued desire to restore repentant national Israel. However, the *leadership* of Israel refused to repent.

> 1 In those days came John the Baptist, preaching in the wilderness of Judaea, 2 And saying, Repent ye: for the kingdom of heaven is at hand. 3 For this is he that was spoken of by the prophet Esaias, saying, The voice of one crying in the wilderness, Prepare ye the way of the Lord, make his paths straight. 4 And the same John had his raiment of camel's hair, and a leathern girdle about his loins; and his meat was locusts and wild honey. 5 Then went out to him Jerusalem, and all Judaea, and all the region round about Jordan, 6 And were baptized of him in Jordan, confessing their sins. 7 But when he saw many of the Pharisees and Sadducees come to his baptism, he said unto them, O generation of vipers, who hath warned you to flee from the wrath to come? 8 Bring forth therefore fruits meet for repentance: 9 And think not to say within yourselves, We have Abraham to *our* father: for I say unto you, that God is able of these stones to raise up children unto Abraham. 10 And now also the axe is laid unto the root of the trees: therefore every tree which bringeth not forth good fruit is

hewn down, and cast into the fire. [11] I indeed baptize you with water unto repentance: but he that cometh after me is mightier than I, whose shoes I am not worthy to bear: he shall baptize you with the Holy Ghost, and *with* fire: [12] **Whose fan *is* in his hand, and he will throughly purge his floor, and gather his wheat into the garner; but he will burn up the chaff with unquenchable fire** (Matthew 3:1-12).

In Matthew 3:12, Jesus is dealing with delusion and the deluded, separating sinners from saints. The point here is that at the time of the second coming of Jesus to the Earth to establish His Kingdom, He is going to *clean house*. The metaphor of separating the wheat from the chaff would have been very familiar to all those living when Jesus said these things. Jesus is speaking about the harvest of His second coming. All Church Age believers will be caught away in the first phase of the harvest. We know this as the Rapture of the Church. At the beginning of the seven-year Tribulation, there will only be lost people left of Earth. Some of these will realize they missed the Rapture and will trust in Christ and be "born again." Since the Tribulation is primarily for the purpose of the restoration and revival of national Israel, the separation metaphor is primarily for Jews. The "wheat" are the Jews who will trust Jesus as their Messiah. The "chaff" are those that will continue to reject Him. Gentiles will be saved too, but this is incidental to this text about Jews.

Understanding this historical and prophetic context, we can understand the statements of Joel 2:32a and Romans 10:13. God was allowing *individual* deliverance and salvation to "whoever," Jew or Gentile, was willing to repent, believe, and call unto Jehovah for salvation. In Romans 10:13, the Word of God is telling us that Jehovah's name is now Jesus. Any individual, either Jew or Gentile, could call upon the name of Jesus confessing Him as LORD and be saved from God's judgment and damnation. This message was part of Peter's message on the Day of Pentecost in Acts chapter two and Peter's second message to the rulers and leaders of Israel in Acts chapter four.

And it shall come to pass that **whosoever** shall call on the name of the Lord shall be saved (Acts 2:21).

[1] And as they spake unto the people, **the priests, and the captain of the temple, and the Sadducees**, came upon them, [2] Being grieved that they taught the people, and preached through Jesus the resurrection from the dead. [3] And they laid hands on them, and put *them* in hold unto the next day: for it was now eventide. [4] Howbeit many of them which heard the word believed; and the number of the men was about five thousand. [5] And it came to pass on the morrow, **that their rulers, and elders, and scribes, [6] And Annas the high priest, and Caiaphas, and John, and Alexander, and as many as were of the kindred of the high priest, were gathered together at Jerusalem**. [7] And when they had set them in the midst, they asked, By what power, or by what name, have ye done this? [8] Then Peter, filled with the Holy Ghost, said unto them, **Ye rulers of the people, and elders of Israel**, [9] If we this day be examined of the good deed done to the impotent man, by what means he is made whole; [10] Be it known unto you all, and to all the people of Israel, that by the name of Jesus Christ of Nazareth, whom ye crucified, whom God raised from the dead, *even* by him doth this man stand here before you whole. [11] This is the stone which was set at nought of you builders, which is become the head of the corner. [12] **Neither is there salvation in any other: for there is none other name under heaven given among men, whereby we must be saved** (Acts 4:1-12).

We cannot separate the mission of the Church corporate and every local church of Jesus Christ from the mission of proclaiming the message of the Gospel to the "Jew first."

For I am not ashamed of the gospel of Christ: for it is the power of God unto salvation to every one that believeth; to the Jew first, and also to the Greek (Romans 1:16).

[4] Or despisest thou the riches of his goodness and forbearance and longsuffering; not knowing that the goodness of God leadeth thee to repentance? [5] But after thy hardness and impenitent heart treasurest up unto thyself wrath against the day of wrath and revelation of the righteous

> judgment of God; [6] Who will render to every man according to his deeds: [7] To them who by patient continuance in well doing seek for glory and honour and immortality, eternal life: [8] But unto them that are contentious, and do not obey the truth, but obey unrighteousness, indignation and wrath, [9] Tribulation and anguish, upon every soul of man that doeth evil, of the Jew first, and also of the Gentile; [10] But glory, honour, and peace, to every man that worketh good, to the Jew first, and also to the Gentile: [11] For there is no respect of persons with God (Romans 2:4-11).

A unity of a group of people from all nations, cultures, and ethnicities is created when individuals from all these nations, cultures, and ethnicities recognize through faith the Person and work of Jesus Christ. That unity is called "the regeneration" (the *again genesis*). During the dispensation of the Church Age, "the regeneration" is called the Church.

> [27] Then answered Peter and said unto him, Behold, we have forsaken all, and followed thee; **what shall we have therefore**? [28] And Jesus said unto **them**, Verily I say unto you, That ye which have followed me, **in the regeneration** when the Son of man shall sit in the throne of his glory, ye also shall sit upon twelve thrones, judging the twelve tribes of Israel. [29] And every one that hath forsaken houses, or brethren, or sisters, or father, or mother, or wife, or children, or lands, for my name's sake, shall receive an hundredfold, and shall inherit everlasting life. [30] But many *that are* first shall be last; and the last *shall be* first (Matthew 19:27-30).

Anyone ("whosoever") can enter "the regeneration" by being "born again" of the Spirit of God. Being "born again" of the Spirit of God does not come by keeping the Commandments (Moralism) or through participation in some religious ritual (Ritualism). Being "born again" of the Spirit of God is a supernatural regeneration of a sinner into a saint in the eyes of God in the instant that sinner repents of sin, believes the objective facts of the "finished" work of Jesus in His dearth, burial, and resurrection, confesses Jesus to be Jehovah God in human flesh, calls on Him to save their souls, and receives Him as the Lord of their lives. There is no other Name and no other Way.

> Unto the church of God which is at Corinth, to them that are sanctified in Christ Jesus, called to be saints, with all that in every place call upon the name of Jesus Christ, our Lord, both theirs and ours (I Corinthians 1:2).

> [5] Thomas saith unto him, Lord, we know not whither thou goest; and how can we know the way? [6] Jesus saith unto him, I am the way, the truth, and the life: <u>no man cometh unto the Father, but by me</u> (John 14:5-6).

Questions for Discussion

1. Discuss why repenting of sin and "dead works," understanding and believing the Gospel, and confessing Jesus as Lord do not save us until we *call* on Jesus to save us.

2. Thoroughly discuss why it is critical to understand the statement in Deuteronomy 11:1-32 that the "righteousness which is of the law" (Romans 10:5) referred to the *national* righteousness of national Israel for God's blessing upon the nation and not to salvational righteousness.

3. Discuss why calling on the name of the Lord Jesus to save must be preceded by repentance of sin and "dead works," understanding and believing the Gospel, and understanding that Jesus is Jehovah God incarnate in human flesh. Then discuss why there must be a certain order in the verb events before a person can be led to the final verb event of being "born again" by calling on the name of the Lord.

4. Discuss why understanding who Jesus is, in the context of confessing, calling, and receiving Him, is critical to comprehending God's expectations of the believing sinner. Discuss how *Only Believism* and *Easy Believism* corrupt this intent.

5. Discuss the context of Joel 2:32 and how this context further explains what it means to call on the name of the Lord Jesus to be saved.

Chapter Nine

Receiving Christ

It is obvious from every Scripture text referenced that confessing, calling, and receiving Jesus is about His Lordship. In other words, the believing sinner confesses with his mouth that Jesus is *Jehovah incarnate* – LORD! The believing sinners then calls upon the name of Jesus as LORD to be saved. The Lordship of Jesus is obviously the context of receiving Jesus in John 1:11-12.

Receiving Christ is both an *identification* and an *association*. The believer identifies himself as the loyal subject of Lord Jesus and affirms his association with Jesus by being an obedient servant to Him and to those He came to redeem. To receive Jesus is to accept Him for Who He is thereby understanding that to do so means reverential worship, subservience, and a consuming desire to live before Him in practical holiness. To receive Christ is to receive the indwelling Person of the Holy Spirit of Christ whereby Jesus lives in us and through us.

> [1] In the beginning was the Word, and the Word was with God, and the Word was God. [2] The same was in the beginning with God. [3] All things were made by him; and without him was not any thing made that was made. [4] In him was life; and the life was the light of men. [5] And the light shineth in darkness; and the darkness comprehended it not. [6] There was a man sent from God, whose name *was* John. [7] The same came for a witness, to bear witness of the Light, that all *men* through him might believe. [8] He was not that Light, but *was sent* to bear witness of that Light. [9] *That* was the true Light, which lighteth every man that cometh into the world. [10] He {*Jehovah incarnate in Jesus*} was in the world, and the world was made by him, and the world knew him not. [11] He came unto his own {*plural neuter gender, therefore referring to His own land and temple*}, and his own {*masculine gender, therefore referring to His own chosen*

people the nation of Israel} received {*paralambano; to take to one's side as an associate or partner in an endeavor*} him not. [12] But as many {*this refers to the 'whosoever' of Romans 10:13*} as received {*lambano*} him, to them gave he power {*authority*} to become {*in 'the regeneration'; i.e. glorification*} the sons of God, *even* to them that believe on his name {*Jesus or Jehovah saves; Matthew 1:21*}: [13] Which were born, not of blood, nor of the will of the flesh, nor of the will of man, but of God {*not a physical birth, but spiritual*}. [14] And the Word was made flesh, and dwelt among us, (and we beheld his glory, the glory as of the only begotten of the Father,) full of grace and truth (John 1:1-14).

When seeking to understand John 1:11-12, we must first ask who is the "he" of verse eleven. Context determines who "he" is. From John 1:1-5, we can see that the "he" of verse eleven is the eternal self-existing Son of God, who is the Creator of the world and the Giver of life. In other words, the "he" of John 1:11 is Jehovah incarnate in the Person of Jesus Christ. To receive Jesus is to receive Jehovah incarnate in the Person of Jesus the promised Redeemer/Messiah of God. Therefore, to receive Jesus is to receive Him as LORD. We can add considerable context to John 1:1-14 with the prophecy of Isaiah 5:1-7.

[1] Now will I sing to my wellbeloved {*Jehovah*} a song of my beloved {*Jehovah's love song regarding*} touching his vineyard {*the land of Israel with the people of Israel as the fruit of the vines planted there*}. My wellbeloved {*Jehovah*} hath a vineyard in a very fruitful hill: [2] And he {*Jehovah*} fenced it {*with a stone wall as a hedge of protection; see vs. 5*}, and gathered out the stones thereof, and planted it with the choicest vine {*the chosen children of Israel; His people*}, and built a tower {*to watch over and guard*} in the midst of it, and also made a winepress therein: and he looked that it should bring forth grapes, and it brought forth wild grapes {*The wild vine looked like grapes but was counterfeit and poisonous. This speaks of the failure of spiritual procreation from one generation to the next. The point being that the vineyard had been corrupted*}. [3] And now, O inhabitants of

> Jerusalem, and men of Judah, judge, I pray you, betwixt me and my vineyard. [4] What could have been done more to my vineyard, that I have not done in it? wherefore, when I looked that it should bring forth grapes, brought it forth wild grapes {*the failure was not God's failure, but rather the failure of the priesthood to teach and the families to learn and teach to their children*}? [5] And now go to; I will tell you what I will do to my vineyard: I will take away the hedge thereof, and it shall be eaten up; *and* break down the wall thereof, and it shall be trodden down: [6] And I will lay it waste: it shall not be pruned, nor digged; but there shall come up briers and thorns: I will also command the clouds that they rain no rain upon it. [7] **For the vineyard of the LORD {*Jehovah*} of hosts *is* the house of Israel, and the men of Judah his pleasant plant**: and he looked for judgment {*the outcome being justice*}, but behold oppression {*the shedding of blood implying injustice*}; for righteousness {*everyone doing what God commanded and therefore order*}, but behold a cry {*clamor, disorder, and anarchy*} (Isaiah 5:1-7).

The context of Isaiah 5:1-7 brings numerous considerations about **receiving Christ** in both an *identification* and an *association.* This connects the **receiving believer** to *responsibility* and *accountability* to the Person he receives. There was supposed to be a *synergism*, a *cooperative partnership*, with God between the *Vine* and the *branches* (also defined in John 15:1-8). This is the intent of the connection in Isaiah 5:1-7 of the *vines* (believers) to the *Branch* (Messiah) to the *Vineyard* (God's family of a community of believers holding one another accountable to obedience to the Law in the promised land of Israel).

Another metaphor is the Olive Tree metaphor that presents the Messiah Jesus as Jehovah incarnate. This metaphor is important because it iss intended is to reflect the relationship of the believer who has received the Lord Jesus, thereby reflecting a spiritual *connection* to the Lord. The *connection* is the outcome of receiving Jesus as Lord. In other words, there are expected *outcomes* of accepting Jesus as Lord in both the Olive Tree and the Vineyard metaphor as believers are spiritually connected to the Branch of the Olive Tree or the Vine in the Vineyard.

> 1 And there shall come forth a rod out of the stem {*The stump that is left after the cutting down of the tree; which cutting down is the chastisement of national Israel showing that God had not cast away His people, Romans 11:1.*} of Jesse, and a Branch {*the incarnate Jehovah in the Messiah*} shall grow out of his roots {*represented in the Candlestick or the Temple Menorah; Exodus 25:31-35 and Revelations 1:20*}: 2 And the spirit of the LORD {*Jehovah*} shall rest upon him, the spirit of wisdom and understanding, the spirit of counsel and might, the spirit of knowledge and of the fear of the LORD; 3 And shall make him of quick understanding in the fear of the LORD: and he shall not judge after the sight of his eyes, neither reprove after the hearing of his ears {*He is the Omniscient Jehovah incarnate; therefore, He will know without seeing or hearing.*}: 4 But with righteousness shall he judge the poor, and reprove with equity for the meek of the earth: and he shall smite the earth with the rod of his mouth, and with the breath of his lips shall he slay the wicked {*during the Kingdom Age defining what it means to rule with a 'rod of iron,' Revelation 2:27 and 12:5*}. 5 And righteousness shall be the girdle of his loins, and faithfulness the girdle of his reins (Isaiah 11:1-5).

Every local church during the Church Age is to be an *embryonic representation* of the rule of Christ during the Kingdom Age. Two governing factors define the rule of the Lord Jesus with His "rod of iron" – "righteousness" and "faithfulness" (Isaiah 11:5). "Righteousness" is to judge between what is right in the eyes of God and what is wrong in the eyes of God. The judgement between right and wrong defines justices. "Faithfulness" simply refers to fidelity to Truth, i.e. the inspired Words of God. Therefore, knowledge of God's Word is the first prerequisite to being faithful to God's Word. It was the work of the priests to insure the *sheep* under their care were instructed in the Word of God and that they lived what they knew. Failure in this responsibility was the reason God's condemnation came upon the corrupted Levitical priesthood of the Mosaic Covenant as detailed in Jeremiah 23:1-6. It is the Levitical priesthood of the nation of Israel that has been cast aside by God, not the nation of Israel.

All Church Age believers are a new Melchisedecan priesthood under their High Priest Jesus Christ. This Melchisedecan priesthood under the Lord Jesus as the believers' High Priest is the context of these glorified believers ruling and reigning with Jesus with a "rod of iron" during the Kingdom Age.

> [26] And **he** that overcometh, and keepeth my works unto the end {*conditions*}, to **him** will I give power over the nations:
> [27] And **he** shall rule them with a rod of iron; as the vessels of a potter shall they be broken to shivers: even as I received of my Father. [28] And I will give **him** the morning star. [29] He that hath an ear, let him hear what the Spirit saith unto the churches (Revelations 2:26-29).

> [11] And I saw heaven opened, and behold a white horse; and he that sat upon him *was* called Faithful and True {*'faithfulness;' Isaiah 11:5*}, and in righteousness {*Isaiah 11:5*} he doth judge and make war. [12] His eyes *were* as a flame of fire, and on his head *were* many crowns; and he had a name written, that no man knew, but he himself. [13] And he *was* clothed with a vesture dipped in blood: and his name is called **The Word of God**. [14] And the armies *which were* in heaven followed him upon white horses, clothed in fine linen {*the new Melchisedecan priesthood of all Church Age believers*}, white and clean. [15] And out of his mouth goeth a sharp sword, that with it he should smite the nations: and **he shall rule them with a rod of iron** {*through and with His new priesthood*}: and he treadeth the winepress of the fierceness and wrath of Almighty God. [16] And he hath on *his* vesture and on his thigh a name written, KING OF KINGS, AND LORD OF LORDS {*Jesus' new Melchisedecan priesthood of all Church Age believers will be the kings of which He is King and the lords of which He is Lord.*} (Revelations 19:11-16).

This context defines what it means to receive Jesus Christ as Lord. The believer *receives* Jesus as the Lord and King thereby connecting the believer to all the privileges and responsibilities of the New Covenant Melchisedecan Priesthood.

This includes the responsibilities to live in righteousness and fidelity to the Words of God as "joint-heirs with Christ" (Romans 8:17, Galatians 3:29). Included in the responsibility of fidelity ("faithfulness") to the Word of God is the responsibility to study the Word of God (II Timothy 2:15) and to know how to apply the knowledge/wisdom gained to every situation of life to maintain personal holiness. This is where the Mosaic Covenant priesthood failed.

> 1 Woe be unto the pastors {*corrupted priesthood*} that
> destroy and scatter the sheep of my pasture! saith the LORD.
> 2 Therefore thus saith the LORD God of Israel against the
> pastors that feed my people; Ye have scattered my flock, and
> driven them away, and have not visited them: behold, I will
> visit upon you the evil of your doings, saith the LORD. 3 And
> I will gather the remnant of my flock out of all countries
> whither I have driven them {*dispersal of the Jews during the*
> *'time of the gentiles'*}, and will bring them again to their
> folds {*back to the Promised Land, Zion*}; and they shall be
> fruitful and increase. 4 And I will set up shepherds over them
> which shall feed them: and they shall fear no more, nor be
> dismayed, neither shall they be lacking, saith the LORD. 5
> Behold, the days come, saith the LORD, that I will raise unto
> David a righteous Branch, and a King shall reign and
> prosper, and shall execute judgment and justice in the earth
> {*Messiah as High Priest, Prophet, and King*}. 6 In his days
> Judah shall be saved, and Israel shall dwell safely: and this
> *is* his name whereby he shall be called, THE LORD OUR
> RIGHTEOUSNESS (Jeremiah 23:1-6).

When we receive Jesus Christ, we *identify* with Him as our personal Lord. This *identification* demands that we *identify* ourselves as His *subjects responsible* to obey His commands. This *responsibility* also defines the believer's *association* with Christ as our High Priest and we as His ministering/servant priests. Within this *identification* and *association*, we have numerous levels of *responsibilities* for which believers are *accountable* to the Lord Jesus. Receiving Jesus as Lord has numerous connotations significant to sovereignty in the Lordship of Jesus. These connotations cannot be separated from the terminology. Understanding this meaning should affect the way we live.

> [11] I say then, Have they {*national Israel*} stumbled that they should fall? God forbid: but *rather* through their fall salvation *is come* unto the Gentiles, for to provoke them to jealousy. [12] Now if the fall of them *be* the riches of the world, and the diminishing of them the riches of the Gentiles; how much more their fullness {*in the restoration of national Israel during the Kingdom Age*}? [13] For I speak to you Gentiles, inasmuch as I am the apostle of the Gentiles, I magnify mine office: [14] If by any means I may provoke to emulation {*excite to rivalry*} *them which are* my flesh, and might save some of them. [15] For if the casting away of them *be* the reconciling of the world, what *shall* the receiving *of them be*, but life from the dead? [16] For if the firstfruit *be* holy {*of glorification in Jesus first than the 'church of the firstborn,' Hebrews 12:23*}, the lump *is* also *holy*: and if the root *be* holy, so *are* the branches. [17] And if some of the branches be broken off, and thou, being a wild olive tree, wert graffed in among them, and with them partakest of the root and fatness of the olive tree; [18] Boast not against the branches. But if thou boast, thou bearest not the root, but the root thee. [19] Thou wilt say then, The branches were broken off, that I might be graffed in. [20] Well; because of unbelief they were broken off, and thou standest by faith. Be not highminded, but fear: [21] For if God spared not the natural branches, *take heed* lest he also spare not thee (Romans 11:11-21).

On the Day of Pentecost, recorded in Acts chapter two, God began a new Dispensation known as the Church Age or the Dispensation of Grace. At this time, natural Israel (or national Israel) was set aside for time span of the whole Church Age. The Day of Pentecost was a *new beginning* (referred to as the New Covenant) in the Abrahamic Covenant. In Romans 11:15-21, God uses the "Olive Tree" metaphorically to represent natural Israel. God cut natural Israel *back to the stump,* or *the root,* to begin again.

The "root" that God *cut back* to is the "Seed," which is Jesus Christ (Galatians 3:16).

The primary purpose of Romans 11:15-24 is a warning to Church Age believers. During the Church Age, God is formulating a new Priesthood of all believers "born again" during this span of time. The faithfulness of Church Age believers is being tested and proven before they will be consecrated to their "holy" and royal" priesthood by their High Priest, Jesus Christ, at the beginning of the Kingdom Age.

The warning of Romans 11:11-21 is that just as the Mosaic priesthood of national/natural Israel was "cut off" due to apostasy, individuals in local churches will also be "cut off" if they fall into apostasy or unfaithfulness to the Great Commission and its intended purpose in making disciples to the glory of God. The seven epistles of Christ to the seven local churches in Revelation 2:1 through 3:22 give us the progressive movement toward this apostasy of the Church. At the end of the Church Age there will be a remnant of faithful local churches, but their numbers will be small.

The warning of Romans 11:17-24 is written to believing Gentiles who have been put into the place of *blessing* in the Abrahamic Covenant "by grace through faith." The warning is given to *individual* Gentile believers of the Church Age, who are prone to forget that they serve a holy God, and a just God, and who forget that they are given moral responsibilities in both knowing the Word of God, teaching the Word of God, and living the Word of God as *believer priests* before God.

> [4] To whom coming, *as unto* a living stone, disallowed indeed of men, but chosen of God, *and* precious, [5] Ye also, as lively stones, are built up a spiritual house, **an holy priesthood**, to offer up spiritual sacrifices, acceptable to God by Jesus Christ. [6] Wherefore also it is contained in the scripture, Behold, I lay in Sion a chief corner stone, elect, precious: and he that believeth on him shall not be confounded. [7] Unto you therefore which believe *he is* precious: but unto them which be disobedient {*apostate natural Israel*}, the stone which the builders disallowed, the same is made the head of the corner {*by God*}, [8] And a stone of stumbling, and a rock

> of offence, *even to them* which stumble at the word, being disobedient: whereunto also they were appointed. [9] But ye {*Church Age believers*} *are* a **chosen generation, a royal priesthood, an holy nation, a peculiar people**; that ye should shew forth the praises of him who hath called you out of darkness into his marvellous light: [10] Which in time past *were* not a people, but *are* now the people of God: which had not obtained mercy, but now have obtained mercy. [11] Dearly beloved, I beseech *you* as strangers and pilgrims, abstain from fleshly lusts, which war against the soul; [12] Having your conversation honest among the Gentiles: that, whereas they speak against you as evildoers, they may by *your* good works, which they shall behold, glorify God in the day of visitation (I Peter 2:4-12).

God also had warned the children of Israel about their similar responsibilities on numerous occasions. Yet they failed to take heed to those warnings and instead killed the prophets that delivered the warnings to them. In the Church Age, this *watching* and *warning* ministry falls primarily upon the shoulders of pastors, but also upon deacons, and evangelists (Acts 20:27-31; Ephesians 4:11). The intent is that this will be reproduced in and through the lives of all faithful believers as they "contend for the faith which was once delivered unto the saints" (Jude 1:3).

> [1] Hear the word of the LORD, ye children of Israel: for the LORD hath a controversy with the inhabitants of the land, because *there is* no truth, nor mercy, nor knowledge of God in the land. [2] By swearing, and lying, and killing, and stealing, and committing adultery, they break out, and blood toucheth blood. [3] Therefore shall the land mourn, and every one that dwelleth therein shall languish, with the beasts of the field, and with the fowls of heaven; yea, the fishes of the sea also shall be taken away. [4] Yet let no man strive, nor reprove another: for thy people *are* as they that strive with the priest. [5] Therefore shalt thou fall in the day, and the prophet also shall fall with thee in the night, and I will destroy thy mother. [6] My people are destroyed for lack of knowledge: because thou hast rejected knowledge, I will

> also reject thee, that thou shalt be no priest to me: seeing thou
> hast forgotten the law of thy God, I will also forget thy
> children. 7 As they were increased, so they sinned against
> me: *therefore* will I change their glory into shame. 8 They eat
> up the sin of my people, and they set their heart on their
> iniquity. 9 And there shall be, **like people, like priest**: and I
> will punish them for their ways, and reward them their
> doings. 10 For they shall eat, and not have enough: they shall
> commit whoredom, and shall not increase: **because they**
> **have left off to take heed to the LORD**. 11 Whoredom and
> wine and new wine take away the heart {*This phraseology refers to the Assyrian Empire's practices in a form of paganism. These practices involved licentious orgies of drunkenness to which the children of Israel had been seduced into involvement in this wickedness before the eyes of God.*} (Hosea 4:1-11).

Confessing Jesus to be Jehovah incarnate, calling on the name of the Lord Jesus to be saved, and receiving Jesus as Lord connects the "born again" believer to the moral responsibilities of their *association* with the Lord Jesus. *Fulfilling* these obligations is not part of what is necessary to receive the gift of salvation. To receive Jesus as Lord is to understand that these moral obligations are certainly expected of those that are redeemed. Adherence to moral obligations should result in a manifestation of moral adherence. This is what defines true *conversion.* Corruption of what it means to receive Jesus as Lord has resulted in *professed conversions* with any *converting* of lifestyle or practices to correspond with being subjects of the Lord. These are false *conversions*.

In Acts chapter three, Peter shows the practical outcome of John 1:11; "He came unto his own, and his own received him not." The context of Acts 3:12-21 provides considerable context to the meaning of receiving the Lord Jesus Christ. This record of Peter's message to the Christ-rejecting Jews is after some undisclosed time from his previous message to the Jews on the Day of Pentecost in Acts chapter two. Peter and John are instrumental in healing a man laying "at the gate of the temple (Acts 3:2). The unbelieving Jews give them credit for the healing of the man. Peter uses the opportunity to confront their consent to, and guilt of, the Messiah's crucifixion.

> 12 And when Peter saw *it*, he answered unto the people, Ye men of Israel, why marvel ye at this? or why look ye so earnestly on us, as though by our own power or holiness we had made this man to walk? 13 The God of Abraham, and of Isaac, and of Jacob, the God of our fathers, hath glorified his Son Jesus; **whom ye delivered up, and denied him in the presence of Pilate**, when he was determined to let *him* go. 14 **But ye denied the Holy One** {*a common phrase in the Old Testament for Jehovah as Saviour, Isaiah 43:3*} **and the Just, and desired a murderer to be granted unto you; 15 And killed the Prince of life** {*the Author or Architect of life, the Creator,; Ephesians 3:9, Colossians 1:16-17*}, whom God hath raised from the dead; whereof we are witnesses. 16 And his name through faith in his name hath made this man strong, whom ye see and know: yea, the faith which is by him hath given him this perfect soundness in the presence of you all. 17 And now, brethren, I wot that through ignorance ye did *it*, as *did* also your rulers. 18 But those things, which God before had shewed by the mouth of all his prophets, that Christ should suffer {*Psalm 22 and Isaiah 53*}, he hath so fulfilled. 19 **Repent ye therefore, and be converted**, that your sins may be blotted out, when the times of refreshing shall come from the presence of the Lord; 20 And he shall send Jesus Christ {*Jesus will establish His Kingdom and Lordship at His second coming*}, which before was preached unto you: 21 Whom the heaven must receive until the times of restitution of all things, which God hath spoken by the mouth of all his holy prophets since the world began (Acts 3:12-21).

Genuine conversion is **always** apparent in progressive change and spiritual growth in progressive transformation. The Greek word *epistrepho* (ep-ee-stref'-o), translated "converted" in Acts 3:19, literally means *to be turned around.* This "conversion" cannot happen apart from genuine repentance. Repentance is the beginning point of that *turning around.* Peter makes this distinction in Acts 3:19; "Repent ye therefore, and be converted, that your sins may be blotted out . . ." Each of the other four verbs in a faith decision also reflect a *turning around* about what we think and believe.

The defining factor in the corruption known as *Lordship Salvation* is that in *Lordship Salvation* the Gospel is *top loaded* with moral obligations to be saved. Many, who claim to believe in *Lordship Salvation,* really do not believe that these obligations are part of salvation. This latter group of people would simply say that to receive the Lord Jesus includes the obligations of discipleship that *accompany* the gift of salvation. This is certainly true, but the obligations of discipleship that *accompany* the gift of salvation are not part of a Bible response to be "born again." The obligations of discipleship that *accompany* the gift of salvation certainly should become evident as the "born again" believer grows "in grace, and *in* the knowledge of our Lord and Saviour Jesus Christ" (II Peter 3:18).

> 11 *Seeing* then *that* all these things shall be dissolved, **what**
> **manner *of persons* ought ye to be in *all* holy conversation**
> **and godliness,** 12 Looking for and hasting unto the coming
> of the day of God, wherein the heavens being on fire shall be
> dissolved, and the elements shall melt with fervent heat? 13
> Nevertheless we, according to his promise, look for new
> heavens and a new earth, wherein dwelleth righteousness. 14
> Wherefore, beloved, seeing that ye look for such things, **be**
> **diligent that ye may be found of him in peace, without**
> **spot, and blameless.** 15 And account *that* the longsuffering
> of our Lord *is* salvation; even as our beloved brother Paul
> also according to the wisdom given unto him hath written
> unto you; 16 As also in all *his* epistles, speaking in them of
> these things; in which are some things hard to be understood,
> which they that are unlearned and unstable wrest, as *they do*
> also the other scriptures, unto their own destruction. 17 Ye
> therefore, beloved, seeing ye know *these things* before,
> beware lest ye also, being led away with the error of the
> wicked, fall from your own stedfastness. 18 **But grow in**
> **grace, and *in* the knowledge of our Lord and Saviour**

Jesus Christ. To him *be* glory both now and for ever. Amen (II Peter 3:11-18).

The words “in grace” in II Peter 3:18 is within the supernatural enabling of the indwelling Lord Jesus in the Person of His Holy Spirit. “In grace” is the believer’s new *standing* (Romans 5:2; *position*) within the New Creation. The Lord Jesus expects His “born again” disciples to progressively “grow” to be more like Him in everything they do. This is the context of Ephesians 2:4-10. Ephesians 2:8-9 are often used to teach salvation to be a “gift” of God. However, there is a failure in making salvation the emphasis of Ephesians 2:4-10. In the progression of Ephesians 2:4 to Ephesians 2:10, the emphasis of the context is upon verse ten.

> [4] But God, who is rich in mercy, for his great love wherewith he loved us, [5] Even when we were dead in sins, **hath quickened us together with Christ**, (by grace ye are saved;) [6] And hath raised *us* up together, and made *us* sit together in heavenly *places* in Christ Jesus: [7] That in the ages to come he might shew the exceeding riches of his grace in *his* kindness toward us through Christ Jesus. [8] For by grace are ye saved {*perfect tense, passive voice, participle mood*} through faith; and that not of yourselves: *it is* the gift of God: [9] Not of works, lest any man should boast. [10] For we are his workmanship, **created in Christ Jesus unto good works**, which God hath before ordained that we should walk in them (Ephesians 2:4-10).

This *collective view* of believers as a local church family is continued from Ephesians chapter one. This *collective responsibility* equates to *collective accountability* both to God and one to another. That this *collective responsibility* is the intent is exemplified in the last three verses of Ephesians chapter two: “[19] Now therefore ye are no more strangers and foreigners, but fellowcitizens with the saints, and of the household {*oikeios – the idea is that of a group of spiritually related people by new birth forming a new living organism as an organized family*} of God {*saved national Israel*}; [20] And are built upon the foundation of the apostles and prophets, Jesus Christ himself being the chief corner *stone*; [21] In whom all the building fitly framed together groweth unto an holy temple in the Lord: [22] In whom ye also are builded together for an habitation of God through the Spirit." Therefore, to receive Christ as Lord connects the believer to a moral responsibility to be united with a local church as a disciple/believer priest.

"*Hath he quickened*" in Ephesians 2:1 is italicized in our KJV, signifying that it is not in the Greek text, but is added for clarification to give us the context. This phrase is added for clarification here because it is the context from Ephesians 2:5. "Were dead in trespasses and sins" refers to the believer's spiritual separation from God prior to his having been spiritually "born again." The first three verses of Ephesians chapter two define the details of what all believers were before they were "quickened" (Ephesians 2:5). We should look carefully at these details because the believer-priest's "walk" should change drastically after he has been "quickened."

God's *collective view* of believer-priests within the context of local church ministries continues in Ephesians 2:4-7. Again, this *collective* context of every local church as a spiritual temple of God is critical to our understanding the moral responsibilities of every believer-priest within the *collective*. There must be a formal uniting to the *collective* and its *communion* in holiness through the promises portrayed through water baptism (Romans 6:1-7).

Water baptism is the formal means through which a believer is formally added to a local assembly of believers to be "perfected for the work of the ministry" (Ephesians 4:12) as a believer/priest. Water baptism has nothing to do with salvation and everything to do with sanctification. The Old Testament type of daily washing the hands and feet of the Levitical priest just prior to his entering into the Temple of God was to begin his cycle of ministry within the Temple priesthood. The warning of death attached to this ritual cleansing of the hands and feet of the priests gives us a grasp upon the seriousness of personal sanctification before ministering before the Lord. Water baptism represents the once for all cleansing of regeneration through the blood of Christ that initiates the believing sinner into the priesthood of the believer in the context of ministering through his local church. I John 1:9

is the verse that gives the believer/priest the context for the daily cleansing of his sin that is like the daily washings of the hands and feet of the priests in the Old Covenant. To receive Christ as Lord connects the believer to this context of his new existence as a believer/priest under his High Priest Jesus Christ. The local church is an accountability group of priests holding one another accountable to personal sanctification.

> [17] And the LORD spake unto Moses, saying, [18] Thou shalt also make a laver *of* brass, and his foot *also of* brass, to wash *withal*: and **thou shalt put it between the tabernacle of the congregation and the altar**, and thou shalt put water therein. [19] For Aaron and his sons **shall wash their hands and their feet thereat**: [20] When they go into the tabernacle of the congregation, they shall wash with water, that they die not; or **when they come near to the altar to minister**, to burn offering made by fire unto the LORD: [21] So they shall wash their hands and their feet, **that they die not**: and it shall be a statute for ever to them, *even* to him and to his seed throughout their generations (Exodus 30:17-21).

Because of the failure of the priesthood of Israel, the nation of Israel had completely lost the message of the Gospel in the Law. They lost the very concept of practical holiness and began to intermarry with the pagans and adopt the customs of the nations (worldliness). Nonetheless, even in God's national chastisement upon Israel, God continued to proclaim His love for His chosen nation through the prophets. Therefore, it is critical that we do not disconnect Ephesians 2:3-10 from Paul's statement in Ephesians 2:12-13. Church Age believers become part of the Abrahamic Covenant "by grace through faith." This phrase in Ephesians 2:8 is a reference to the Abrahamic Covenant and the offer of salvation to "whosoever."

In Matthew 21:33, Jesus is speaking to "the chief priests and the elders of the people" who came to question Jesus "by what authority" He performed miracles (Matthew 21:23). They were asking Jesus from where He got the ability to perform the miracles. The Scribes and Pharisees of Israel had been accusing Jesus of doing these miracles by the power of "Beelzebub" (Matthew

12:24; Mark 3:22). The parable is addressed to priesthood of Israel spoken of in the prophecy of Isaiah 5:1-7.

The individuals to whom Jesus was giving this parable of Matthew 21:33-46 would have understood that He was referring to Isaiah's prophecy. They also would know that the parable was being applied to them specifically. They would know and understand that the substance of the parable was about them rejecting the Lordship of the Lord Jesus over the household of national Israel. This is the context of John 1:11-12. Although the priesthood of Israel rejected the Lord Jesus as their Lord, and thereby *at that time* rejected His Kingdom, any ("as many") individuals that "received" Him as Lord would be given the authority to call themselves the "sons of God" (John 1:12). This defines the "whosoever" in the offer of the gift of salvation.

> 33 Hear another parable: There was a certain **householder**
> {*Jehovah, Isaiah 5:1-7*}, which planted a **vineyard** {*the*
> *nation of Israel*}, and hedged it round about, and digged a
> winepress in it, and built a tower, and **let it out** {*leased it*
> *expecting a portion of the fruit in return*} to **husbandmen**
> {*the Priesthood of Israel into whose care the nation of Israel*
> *had been assigned*}, and went into a far country: 34 And
> when the time of the fruit drew near, he sent **his servants**
> {*most likely the prophets of God coming expecting fruit from*
> *the Vineyard*} to the **husbandmen**, that they might receive
> the fruits of it. 35 And the husbandmen {*the corrupted*
> *leaders of Israel*} took his servants, and beat one, and killed
> another, and stoned another. 36 Again, he sent other servants
> more than the first: and they did unto them likewise. 37 But
> last of all he sent unto them his son {*the Messiah Jesus*},
> saying, They will reverence my son. 38 But when the
> husbandmen saw the son, they said among themselves, This
> is the heir {*of the earthly Kingdom*}; come, let us kill him,
> and **let us seize on his inheritance**. 39 And they caught him,
> and cast *him* out of the vineyard, and slew *him*. 40 When the
> lord therefore of the vineyard cometh, what will he do unto
> those husbandmen? 41 They say unto him, He will miserably
> destroy those wicked men, and will let out *his* vineyard unto
> other husbandmen, which shall render him the fruits in their

seasons. [42] Jesus saith unto them, Did ye never read in the scriptures, The stone which the builders rejected, the same is become the head of the corner {*Psalm 118:22-23*}: this is the Lord's doing, and it is marvellous in our eyes? [43] Therefore say I unto you, **The kingdom of God shall be taken from you**, and **given to a nation bringing forth the fruits thereof**. [44] And whosoever shall fall on this stone shall be broken: but on whomsoever it shall fall, it will grind him to powder. [45] And when the chief priests and Pharisees had heard his parables, **they perceived that he spake of them**. [46] But when they sought to lay hands on him, they feared the multitude, because they took him for a prophet (Matthew 21:33-46).

The connotations of the *parable of the Vineyard* in Matthew 21:33-46 (also recorded in Luke 20:9-19) is that the leadership of Israel (the priesthood and king) would reject the Messiah for covetous and selfish reasons. Therefore, the nation of Israel would be momentarily removed as the "husbandmen" of the Vineyard and replaced by "a nation bringing forth the fruits thereof" (Matthew 21:43). This is the new priesthood of all believers during the Church Age through thousands of independent local churches throughout the world. The missional purpose for every one of these local church congregations of priests is "bringing forth the fruits" of God's Vineyard. The central responsibility of the caretakers of the Vineyard is the production of "fruit" to the glory of God. The believer connects himself in *identity* and *association* with the Lord Jesus by receiving Jesus as Lord.

Questions for Discussion

1. Thoroughly discuss how receiving Jesus as Lord corresponds with the following statement: "Receiving Christ is both an *identification* and an *association*."

2. Discuss how understanding John 1:1-4 defines what it means to receive the Person of Jesus Christ in John 1:11-12.

3. Discuss what the context of Isaiah 5:1-7 brings to our understanding of what it means to receive the Lord Jesus Christ.

4. Discuss what the context of Isaiah 11:1-5 brings to our understanding of what it means to receive the Lord Jesus Christ.

5. Discuss what the context of Revelations 2:26-29 and Revelations 19:11-16 brings to our understanding of what it means to receive the Lord Jesus Christ.

Chapter Ten

The Sinner's Prayer

There is no such thing as the *sinner's prayer* in the Bible. I John 1:9 is not defining the *sinner's prayer.* The *sinner's prayer* is not about confessing your sins to God to receive forgiveness. I John 1:9 is about "fellowship" with God (I John 1:3, 6, and 7), not salvation. However, there is prayer that communicates with God about salvation in the phrase "whosoever shall call upon the name of the Lord shall be saved" (Romans 10:13). In other words, calling "upon the name of the Lord" to "be saved" is the *sinner's prayer.* To "call upon the name of the Lord" to "be saved" is simply *accepting/receiving* the gift God offers in His gift of salvation. There is no begging or pleading involved in this communication with God. The *sinner's prayer* is simply telling God you accept His gift offered "by grace . . . through faith" (Ephesians 2:8).

There are those saying that a *prayer* is not necessary for salvation. They say that God simply acts upon His knowledge of the heart of the believing sinner. There are others that say that helping a person with the *sinner's prayer* reduces this prayer to simply saying certain words as if they will *magically* produce salvation. Although these are real concerns, neither of these are applicable to the real substance of the *sinner's prayer* - calling "upon the name of the Lord" to "be saved."

The sinner calling on the name of Jesus to request the gift of salvation does not need to declare that he has completed all the other verbs that define saving faith. The other verbs need be rehearsed to ensure a person understands prior to praying the *sinner's prayer.* Verbs are action words. Therefore, repentance of sin and "dead works" must have already happened prior to praying the *sinner's prayer.* Resting in the understanding of what the Gospel accomplishes God-ward (propitiation) and man-ward (justification) simply must be a reality prior to praying the *sinner's prayer.* These truths define what it means to believe with the heart. If repenting and believing have already happened, reiterating them in the *sinner's prayer* is not required. There is no harm in a person communicating his understanding of repentance and believing in the *sinner's prayer*, but this is not required. The *sinner's prayer* is about *calling* on the Lord Jesus to save (Romans 10:13) and *receiving* the indwelling Jesus as Lord (John 1:11-12).

Confessing with the mouth that Jesus is Lord (Jehovah incarnate) is a public acknowledgement and announcement of the Lordship of Jesus over a person's life. This is not the *sinner's prayer*. The *sinner's prayer* is connected to calling on the Name of the Lord to save the sinner and thereby receive the Lord Jesus Christ in the Person of His indwelling Spirit. To "call upon the name of the Lord" presupposes faith in God's ability and willingness to give what He offers in salvation. *Calling* is certainly not the same as *believing*, even though the verbs are intricately connected.

There is no specific order given in the Bible detailing when these five verbs are expected to take place. However, the ambiguity certainly can be clarified by simple logic. Repentance of sin and "dead works" must precede believing because repentance eliminates any trust in Moralism and Ritualism. Therefore, repentance defines what cannot be believed before what needs to be believed is established. Repentance of sin establishes from what a sinner needs to be saved – condemnation because of sin (Romans 3:23, 5:8, and 12).

Believing the Gospel must be the second verb in the order because understanding what the Gospel of Jesus accomplishes in the propitiation of God and the justification of the sinner is the explanation of how God can save a sinner in the first place. Understanding and believing what the Gospel of Jesus Christ accomplishes on the sinner's behalf is prerequisite to confessing Jesus as Lord, calling on Him to save, and receiving Him as Lord. Although these five verbs are intricately connected to one another in a chain of events, they are not all equal in meaning. The culminating verb that generates the actual event of salvation is the verb "call." The verb "confess" in the phrase "confess the Lord Jesus," is the manifestation of a public identification with Jesus as the believing sinner's Lord. In other words, the faith of the person who calls upon the name of the Lord to be saved will cause God to create a "new creation" in an event that is that person's regeneration – being "born again." The regenerated person will then not hesitate to publicly confess with his mouth that Jesus is Lord.

> 8 But what saith it? The word is nigh thee, *even* in thy mouth,
> and in thy heart: that is, the word of faith, which we preach;
> 9 That if thou shalt confess with thy mouth the Lord Jesus,
> and shalt believe in thine heart that God hath raised him from
> the dead, thou shalt be saved. 10 For with the heart man
> believeth unto righteousness; and with the mouth confession
> is made unto salvation. 11 For the scripture saith, Whosoever
> believeth on him shall not be ashamed. 12 For there is no
> difference between the Jew and the Greek: for the same Lord
> over all is rich unto all that call upon him. 13 For whosoever
> shall call upon the name of the Lord shall be saved. 14 How
> then shall they call on him in whom they have not believed?
> and how shall they believe in him of whom they have not
> heard? and how shall they hear without a preacher (Romans
> 10:8-14)?

Logic would require that calling on the name of Jesus and receiving Jesus as Lord defines the substance of the *sinner's prayer*. This is also supported by Romans 10:14; "How then shall they call on him in whom they have not believed?" Therefore, the *sinner's prayer* is simply communicating to God the sinner's request to be saved and receive the gift of salvation. The gift of salvation is the righteousness of God in the Person of the indwelling Spirit of the Lord Jesus Christ.

The gift of salvation is also the remission of the penalty of sin, which is eternal separation from God (death), and the justification of the sinner (impartation of the righteousness of God in the indwelling divine nature; II Peter 1:4). If the Gospel has been explained adequately and understood adequately, communicating this understanding need not be a part of the substance of the *sinner's prayer*. The *sinner's prayer* is the simple request to be saved that springs forth from a proper understanding of the condemnation of sin and what Jesus accomplished for the sinner that is detailed in the Gospel.

EASY PRAYERISM

There is foolishness in the one, two, three say it after me sinner's prayer. Although there is considerable value to the objections against *Easy Prayerism*, the real objection is about praying a prayer that has no foundation in the prerequisites of genuine repentance and genuine understanding of what the Gospel of the Lord Jesus Christ accomplishes. Therefore, such a prayer would not have the necessary doctrinal foundations that give any substance to faith (Hebrews 11:1). This is what defines *Easy Prayerism.*

The *sinner's prayer* is a simple prayer that comes from the heart uttered out of complete desperation grasping onto a surety of hope in the promised gift of God. The *sinner's prayer* should naturally flow from a thorough understanding of the complete depravation of the sinner's lost condition and a thorough understanding of God's solution to that problem in the accomplishments of the death, burial, resurrection, and glorification of Jesus Christ. The work of the ministry of the evangelist is to explain to insure understanding of repentance and redemption. "How shall they hear without a preacher" (Romans 10:14).

Superficial *sinner's prayers* are the normal outcome of superficial explanations of the doctrines of condemnation and redemption. It would be anachronous (*out of place in time*) to pray to call on the name of the Lord to save before understanding what the Gospel accomplishes for the sinner. It would also be anachronous to confess Jesus to be our Lord if we have not called upon Him as Lord first.

Praying the *sinner's prayer* before repentance and understanding/believing are realities, results in false professions resulting in unconverted people trying to live the *Christ-life*. These people get baptized (often with no understanding of what water baptism means) and join a local church only to *fall away* from "the faith" soon thereafter. This scenario is what Jesus addresses in the parable of the Sower, the Soils, and the Seed.

> 3 And he spake many things unto them in parables, saying,
> Behold, a sower went forth to sow; 4 And when he sowed,

> some *seeds* fell by the way side, and the fowls came and devoured them up: [5] Some fell upon stony places, where they had not much earth: and forthwith they sprung up, because they had no deepness of earth: [6] And when the sun was up, they were scorched; and because they had no root, they withered away. [7] And some fell among thorns; and the thorns sprung up, and choked them: [8] But other fell into good ground, and brought forth fruit, some an hundredfold, some sixtyfold, some thirtyfold. [9] Who hath ears to hear, let him hear (Matthew 13:3-9).

As Jesus explains this parable to His disciples, it is apparent that He is dealing with hypothetical false professions that result from inadequate explanations of the Gospel and what the Gospel accomplishes. It is also apparent that these hypothetical false professors do not understand the evangelistic obligations of the gift of salvation and are powerless to accomplish these expectations because they are not genuinely "born again." Inadequate explanations of the Gospel create a pseudo-faith resulting in people attempting to *self-manufacture* a Christian life. There is little wonder that the outcomes described in Matthew 13:18-22 happen.

> [16] But blessed *are* your eyes, for they see: and your ears, for they hear. [17] For verily I say unto you, That many prophets and righteous *men* have desired to see *those things* which ye see, and have not seen *them*; and to hear *those things* which ye hear, and have not heard *them*. [18] Hear ye therefore the parable of the sower. [19] When any one heareth the word of the kingdom, and **understandeth *it* not**, then cometh the wicked *one*, and catcheth away that which was sown in his heart. This is he which received seed by the way side. [20] But he that received the seed into stony places, the same is he that heareth the word, and anon with joy receiveth it; [21] Yet **hath he not root in himself**, but dureth for a while: for when tribulation or persecution ariseth because of the word, by and by he is offended. [22] He also that received seed among the thorns is he that heareth the word; and the care of this world {*worldliness*}, and the deceitfulness of riches, choke the

word, and he becometh unfruitful {*might be saved, but produces no fruit*}. [23] But he that received seed into the good ground is he that heareth the word, and **understandeth** *it*; which also beareth fruit, and bringeth forth, some an hundredfold, some sixty, some thirty (Matthew 13:16-23).

What Jesus describes in Matthew 13:16-23 is a warning against superficial explanations of the Gospel of Jesus Christ and a superficial explanation of the five verbs that define a genuine faith conversion of the heart. Superficial faith produces a superficial *sinner's prayer* that utters mere words disconnected from a heart filled with conviction and understanding. Jesus probably preached this same parable often and explained it more than once. His explanation in the Gospel of Luke is a different than in Matthew and perhaps a bit more thorough. In Luke, it is apparent that the "good ground" is a convicted and understanding heart described as "honest and good" (Luke 8:15). The *sinner's prayer* must cry out to God for salvation from the heart that lays within the deep conviction and understanding of the need for that salvation. A converted heart can only be conceived when conviction and understanding come together in the sinner's heart. A convicted and understanding heart will supernaturally produce a biblical *sinner's prayer* bursting forth from real faith.

[11] Now the parable is this: The seed is the word of God. [12] Those by the way side are they that hear; then cometh the devil, and taketh away the word out of their hearts, lest they should believe and be saved. [13] They on the rock *are they*, which, when they hear, receive the word with joy; and **these have no root**, which for a while believe, and in time of temptation fall away. [14] And that which fell among thorns are they, which, when they have heard, go forth, and are choked with cares and riches and pleasures of *this* life, and bring no fruit to perfection. [15] But that on the good ground are they, which **in an honest and good heart, having heard the word, keep *it***, and bring forth fruit with patience (Luke 8:11-15).

God's Word says, "The fruit of the righteous *is* a tree of life; and he that winneth souls *is* wise" (Proverbs 11:30). The word "winneth" is translated from the Hebrew word *laqach* (law-kakh'). The word means *to take*, *to carry*, or *to bring*. The intent is to *lead a soul* to the "tree of life" in the Gospel of Jesus Christ. The intent of the word "winneth" is to *direct the heart*, to *win the heart* by persuasively leading the convicted and understanding heart to call upon the Name of Jesus and to receive His indwelling presence so as to be "born again" of the Spirit. Therefore, the soul winner must be both knowledgeable of the Scriptures to explain the Gospel and the biblical responses thereto. The soul winner must also be knowledgeable and discerning in understanding the human heart so as to be careful not to move ahead of the Spirit of God's convicting and giving understanding.

It might be said, a soul winner can lead a sinner *to* the sinner's prayer, but not *through* the sinner's prayer. In other words, the soul winner should not merely put words in the sinner's mouth like a ventriloquist and his dummy. Explaining what the sinner must thoroughly understand about his condemnation and what Jesus has done to thoroughly resolve the problems of condemnation should prompt the sinner to see what is involved in repentance and in believing the Gospel. The believing sinner should be able to communicate that understanding in prayer to God with little help from the soul winner *if that understanding is real*. From there, the sinner needs simply to call on the name of the Lord Jesus to save his soul thereby receiving Jesus as the Lord of his life and will then "confess with the mouth" Jesus as Lord at the very first opportunity.

In Proverbs 11:30, the "righteous" are those who are genuinely saved and are righteous by imputation. Their "fruit" is the "tree of lives," or saved souls. Genuinely "born again" people should produce other genuinely "born again" people. This is to what Jesus alludes in Matthew 13:23 in the words, "beareth fruit, and bringeth forth, some an hundredfold, some sixty, some thirty." The same is true in the words of Luke 8:15; "bring forth fruit with patience." Jesus speaks to this also in John 15:1-8.

> [1] I am the true vine, and my Father is the husbandman. [2]
> **Every branch <u>in me</u> that beareth not fruit he taketh**

away: and every *branch* that beareth fruit, he purgeth it, that it may bring forth more fruit. 3 Now ye are clean through the word which I have spoken unto you. 4 Abide in me, and I in you. As **the branch cannot bear fruit of itself**, except it abide in the vine; no more can ye, except ye abide in me. 5 I am the vine, ye *are* the branches: He that abideth in me, and I in him, **the same bringeth forth much fruit**: for without me ye can do nothing. 6 If a man abide not in me, he is cast forth as a branch, and is withered; and men gather them, and cast *them* into the fire, and they are burned. 7 If ye abide in me, and my words abide in you, ye shall ask what ye will, and it shall be done unto you. 8 **Herein is my Father glorified, that ye bear much fruit; so shall ye be my disciples** (John 15:1-8).

The text is a metaphor using the grape vine and a branch growing from the vine. The metaphor is typical of having been united to Christ and His eternal power and purpose through salvation. Every branch coming forth from the vine is expected to bear fruit. Any branch coming from the vine that does not show any signs of producing fruit is taken away. In other words, it is pruned or cut off from the vine. The branches that show signs of bearing fruit are purged or purified of small branches (*worldliness*) that come forth from them so that they can give all their nutrients drawn from the vine to produce a large, robust cluster of grapes. This cluster of grapes is the winning and discipleship of other souls. These texts (Matthew 13:16-23, Luke 8:11-15, and John 15:1-8) show us that people who do not produce fruit of other saved souls after a profession of faith in Christ is for one of two reasons:

1. They do not have conviction and understanding in their hearts so that when they call on the name of Jesus to be saved, conversion does not take place in their hearts. Therefore, they remain unregenerate (Matthew 13:19-21 and Luke 8:12-13). Although God will bless His Word (Isaiah 55:11) even when it comes forth from the mouths of unregenerate people, these souls are won to Christ *in spite* of these unregenerate people rather than *because* of them.

2. They may get saved but are never taught what is involved in abiding in Christ and living a separated, sanctified, fully surrendered Spirit-filled lives to the glory of God. The person without the commitment to fully surrender to Christ must be *pruned*, not *purged* (Matthew 13:22 and John 15:2).

Teaching these two reasons why people who profess to be saved do not bring others to Christ must be part of the follow-up of a person publicly confessing Christ as Lord. The proper time to explain these things is at the time the confessing sinner comes to a decision to be water baptized and become a formal member of the local church. This is the time for a very careful detailed examination of the believer's heart conviction of sin, his repentance of sin and "dead works" from the heart, his heart understanding of what the Gospel accomplishes, and the explanation of his five verb responses to the Gospel of Jesus Christ from the heart.

There is great danger in giving a lost sinner assurance of a false salvation. This is exactly what Satan wants to happen. This is an issue that will be dealt with extensively in the following chapters. These chapters need to be understood by the evangelist/disciple-maker and carefully explained to the new professing Christian. There is also a grave danger in allowing a person with a false conversion to become a member of a local church. Such a person will need to be constantly *propped up* in just about everything he does because he is still *dead in trespasses and sin.* Every aspect of this person's attempt at Christianity will be discouraging and fruitless. Preaching to such a person will prove hopeless and his Christian life will prove to be artificial and hypocritical. Failing to deal with an obvious façade of real faith is a great injustice against a person that has a false conversion. Doing so is equal to spiritual malpractice.

The significant warning here about baptizing new believers and bringing them into formal church membership is– PROCEED WITH CAUTION! The words of John the Baptist should be carefully applied here – "Bring forth therefore fruits {*ripe picked fruits; i.e., evident maturity*} meet {*comparable, or befitting*} for repentance" (Matthew 3:8).

The *sinner's prayer* should communicate to God the sinner's understanding. Therefore, the *sinner's prayer* should be in the sinner's own words. After the sinner prays, do not hesitate to ask any questions about misunderstandings that are communicated in the prayer. Simply state, *there appears to be some misunderstanding communicated in your prayer and it is important that we ensure that you properly understand.* An example of a *sinner's prayer* might be as follows (do not tell the sinner to *say these words after me*):

> Father, I know that I was born a sinner and have since sinned against you many times. I know that I deserve to be eternally separated from you and condemned to an eternal Hell. I turn from my sins and want to live according to your will. I understand that doing *good works* or participating in some *sacrament* cannot help me to be saved from your wrath. I understand and believe that Jesus has satisfied your wrath upon all my sins when He once and forever bore the death penalty for my sins in His body on the Cross of Calvary. I understand and believe that you will give me the gift of your righteousness to indwell me in the Person of the Holy Spirit when you give me the gift of salvation. Because I believe these truths, I call upon the name of Jesus to save my soul from Hell and give me eternal life. I receive the indwelling presence of Jesus as my Lord and Savior. I will whole heartedly and publicly confess with my mouth Jesus as the Lord of my life and Jehovah incarnate at the next opportunity given me. I pray this in the name of Jesus. Thank you for saving my soul. Amen!

Questions for Discussion

1. Discuss why Romans 10:13 is what really defines the *sinner's prayer.*

2. Discuss what other actions (verbs) need to be completed prior to calling on the name of the Lord to be saved and why these previous actions are essential to calling.

3. Discuss why confessing with the mouth that Jesus is Lord (Jehovah incarnate) in a public acknowledgement and announcement of the Lordship of Jesus over a person's life is not the *sinner's prayer.*

4. Discuss why logic would require that calling on the name of Jesus and receiving Jesus as Lord defines the substance of the *sinner's prayer.*

5. Discuss the difference between leading a person **to** the *sinner's prayer* rather than leading a person **through** the *sinner's prayer.* Then, in your own words, write out what you think should be the **substance** of a *sinner's prayer.*

Chapter Eleven

The Confusion of False Professions

There are many people who profess to be Christians who are not true believers in a biblical sense. Trying to settle the matter of these false professions and issues of pseudo-salvation is not going to happen by discussing if a person is eternally secure in his false profession or if he has lost his salvation. Neither apply to the problem. The problem is that such a person was never "born again" in the first place. False professions should be the focus of the discussion.

The debate between those believing in the eternal security of "born again" believers and those believing that a person can lose his salvation if he abandons his faith in Christ has been ongoing for centuries, if not millennia. Having participated in these discussions for close to fifty years of my life, it seems apparent that people on both side of the issue are talking about the same problem, but are not hearing each other. The reason both sides of this issue do not hear each other is because they BOTH argue from *straw man positions* about the other's beliefs. *Straw man positions* are the extremes of both positions. However, gaining a biblical balance between the extremes is not that difficult if we stop the argument and listen to God's Scriptures.

> 5 For this cause left I thee in Crete, that thou shouldest set in
> order the things that are wanting, and ordain elders in every
> city, as I had appointed thee: 6 If any be blameless, the
> husband of one wife, having faithful children not accused of
> riot or unruly. 7 For a bishop must be blameless, as the
> steward of God; not selfwilled, not soon angry, not given to
> wine, no striker, not given to filthy lucre; 8 But a lover of
> hospitality, a lover of good men, sober, just, holy, temperate;
> 9 Holding fast the faithful word as he hath been taught, that
> he may be able by sound doctrine both to exhort and to
> convince the gainsayers. 10 For there are many unruly and
> vain talkers and deceivers, specially they of the
> circumcision: 11 Whose mouths must be stopped, who

subvert whole houses, teaching things which they ought not, for filthy lucre's sake. [12] One of themselves, *even* a prophet of their own, said, The Cretians *are* alway liars, evil beasts, slow bellies. [13] This witness is true. Wherefore rebuke them sharply, that they may be sound in the faith; [14] Not giving heed to Jewish fables, and commandments of men, that turn from the truth. [15] Unto the pure all things *are* pure: but unto them that are defiled and unbelieving *is* nothing pure; but even their mind and conscience is defiled. [16] They profess that they know God; but in works they deny *him*, being abominable, and disobedient, and unto every good work reprobate (Titus 1:5-16).

First, if someone is going to participate in the theological discussion between eternal security and the belief that a believer can fall away, he must first understand the *straw men* out of which the discussion springs. *The straw men* are the product of two false forms of theology based upon proof texting or Aristotelian Syllogism. Therefore, both arguments are *logical* rather than *theological.*

1. Monergism out of Augustinianism or Calvinism: This is the belief that salvation is completely of God whereby God randomly and *unconditionally* chooses those He will save, regenerates only those individuals giving them faith and repentance before they believe. These *elect* regenerated individuals will not be able to *resist* God's call to them to trust in Christ and will eventually be saved. These individuals will *persevere* unto the end because God is working in them to do so. Those that do not persevere were not of the elect and were never regenerated. This is not the same as the biblical doctrine of eternal security.

2. Synergism out of Arminianism: This is the belief that a person participates in receiving the gift of salvation by a decision of faith. This is true. However, *Arminian synergism* means that this person must also *keep* his own salvation by continuing in "the faith." If a person *falls away* from the faith, he will lose salvation and must be "born again" again.

Neither of these two *straw men positions* are close to what the Bible teaches. The Bible, God's Word, does not talk in the terms of Monergism or Synergism. The problem with these two *logical* arguments is that they establish a *position* and then interpret by using *proof texts* according to that *presupposition.* This methodology corrupts biblical *exegesis* turning it into *eisegesis.* Exegesis essentially means *to lead out of.* In other words, the conclusions *come out of* the text. Eisegesis essentially means *to lead into.* In other words, the conclusions are *introduced into* the text beforehand. Exegesis is honest Bible interpretation. Eisegesis is dishonest Bible interpretation.

The Gospel of Jesus Christ is a declaration of *accomplished,* definitive truths regarding the incarnation of the Son of God, His vicarious death propitiating God's wrath upon the sins of humanity. This finished work of redemption extends from Adam to the end of time. This finished work of redemption involves His burial, and His resurrection/glorification from the dead signifying His victory over Satan's *death grip* on mankind due to the curse. The truth of the Gospel is "it is finished." **If** you have been converted in your heart, you have been saved by the operations of the indwelling Spirit of Christ and your salvation is already "finished" in the eyes of God.

> 4 And this I say, lest any man should beguile you with enticing words. 5 For though I be absent in the flesh, yet am I with you in the spirit, joying and beholding your order, and the stedfastness of your faith in Christ. 6 As ye have therefore received Christ Jesus the Lord, *so* walk ye in him: 7 Rooted and built up in him, and stablished in the faith, as ye have been taught, abounding therein with thanksgiving. 8 Beware lest any man spoil you through philosophy and vain deceit, after the tradition of men, after the rudiments of the world, and not after Christ. 9 For in him dwelleth all the fulness of the Godhead bodily. 10 And **ye are complete in him**, which is the head of all principality and power: 11 In whom also ye are circumcised **with the circumcision made without hands**, in putting off the body of the sins of the flesh by the circumcision of Christ: 12 **Buried with him in {*Spirit*} baptism**, wherein also ye are **risen with *him* through the**

> **faith of the operation of God**, who hath raised him from the dead. [13] And you, being dead in your sins and the uncircumcision of your flesh, **hath he quickened together with him**, having forgiven you all trespasses; [14] Blotting out the handwriting of ordinances that was against us, which was contrary to us, and took it out of the way, nailing it to his cross; [15] *And* having spoiled principalities and powers, he made a shew of them openly, triumphing over them in it (Colossians 2:4-15).

Colossians 2:14-15 defines what has happened to the believer ***positionally*** in the eyes of God **IF** he has truly been "born again" of the Spirit of God. The point is simple. **IF** you have been truly "born again" of the Spirit of God, everything that has happened to the Lord Jesus Christ has *ALREADY positionally* happened to you in the "operation of God" in your salvation (Colossians 2:12). The point in the exegesis of Colossians 2:4-15 is that there are several irreversible acts accomplished in the "operation of God" in a person's salvation. These four operations are regeneration (again genesis), the indwelling of the Spirit of God, the baptism with the Spirit of God, and the sealing of the Spirit of God - sealing is referred to as the "earnest of the Spirit" in II Corinthians 1:22 and II Corinthians 5:5. The word "earnest" is from the Greek word *arrhabon* (ar-hrab-on'), which basically means *security deposit* that guarantees the completion of a purchase.

> **Regeneration**: if a person has been "born again," and could lose his salvation, he would also need to be "un-born again."
> **Indwelling**: the instant a person puts faith in Jesus Christ for salvation, the Holy Spirit indwells him. If he could lose his salvation, the Holy Spirit would have to un-indwell him. Hebrews 13:5 says that He will never do that.
> **The Baptism of the Spirit**: the instant a person puts faith in Jesus Christ for salvation, the Holy Spirit makes that believer a part of the "body of Christ" (I Corinthians 12:13, i.e., the New Creation or part of "the regeneration"). If we could lose our salvation, the Holy Spirit would have to un-join us from the "body of Christ."

The Sealing of the Holy Spirit: the Holy Spirit is said to be the believer's seal of redemption (Ephesians 4:30). If a believer could lose his salvation, he would have to be un-sealed. This would deny Ephesians 4:30 (compare Romans 8:14-23).

However, God's Word frequently speaks in the terms of *false professions* due to misunderstanding and the failure to be *converted in the heart*. One of the clearest Bible texts on the subject is Christ's parable of the Sower and the Soils in Matthew chapter thirteen. It is critically important that we properly exegete this text and avoid any tendency to interject a presupposition into the text. In other words, we want to get what God says *out of* the text. We want to avoid *reading into* the text a preconceived supposition.

> 1 The same day went Jesus out of the house, and sat by the
> sea side. 2 And great multitudes were gathered together unto
> him, so that he went into a ship, and sat; and the whole
> multitude stood on the shore. 3 And he spake many things
> unto them in parables, saying, **Behold, a sower went forth
> to sow**; 4 And when he sowed, some *seeds* fell by the way
> side, and the fowls came and devoured them up: 5 Some fell
> upon stony places, where they had not much earth: and
> forthwith they sprung up, because they had no deepness of
> earth: 6 And when the sun was up, they were scorched; and
> because they had no root, **they withered away**. 7 And some
> fell among thorns; and the thorns sprung up, and **choked
> them**: 8 But other fell into good ground, and brought forth
> fruit, some an hundredfold, some sixtyfold, some thirtyfold.
> **9 Who hath ears to hear, let him hear.** 10 And the disciples
> came, and said unto him, Why speakest thou unto them in
> parables? 11 He answered and said unto them, Because it is
> given unto you to know {*to understand or perceive*} the
> mysteries of the kingdom of heaven, **but to them** {*the
> apostate Jews of the Temple order*} it is not given. 12 For
> whosoever hath, to him shall be given, and he shall have
> more abundance: but whosoever hath not, from him shall be
> taken away even that he hath. 13 Therefore speak I to them

{*the apostate Jews of the Temple order*} in parables: because they seeing see not; and hearing they hear not, neither do they **understand** {*key word to the parable; soon-ee'-ay-mee – to put togeather or comprehend*}. 14 And in them is fulfilled the prophecy of Esaias, which saith, By hearing ye shall hear, and shall not **understand**; and seeing ye shall see, and shall **not perceive**: 15 For this people's heart is waxed gross, and *their* ears are dull of hearing, and their eyes they have closed; lest at any time they should see with *their* eyes, and hear with *their* ears, and should **understand with *their* heart**, and should **be converted** {*to be turned around*}, and I should heal them. 16 But blessed *are* your eyes, for they see: and your ears, for they hear. 17 For verily I say unto you, That many prophets and righteous *men* have desired to see *those things* which ye see, and have not seen *them*; and to hear *those things* which ye hear, and have not heard *them*. 18 **Hear ye therefore the parable of the sower**. 19 When any one heareth the word of the kingdom, and **understandeth *it* not**, then cometh the wicked *one*, and catcheth away that which was sown in his heart. This is he which received seed by the way side. 20 But he that received the seed into stony places, the same is he that heareth the word, and anon with joy receiveth it; 21 Yet hath he **not root in himself** {*no understanding or foundation of real faith*}, but dureth for a while: for when tribulation or persecution ariseth because of the word, by and by he is offended. 22 He also that received seed among the thorns is he that heareth the word; and the care of this world, and the deceitfulness of riches, choke the word, and he becometh unfruitful. 23 But he that received seed into the good ground is he that heareth the word, **and understandeth** *it*; which also beareth fruit, and bringeth forth, some an hundredfold, some sixty, some thirty (Matthew 13:1-23).

A central part of giving the Gospel of Jesus Christ is giving the believer God's directions for responding to the Gospel message to receive God's gift of salvation. **The believer must *understand* ALL THESE truths and respond according to God's**

specifications of faith – REPENT, UNDERSTAND and BELIEVE, CONFESS, CALL, and RECEIVE.

There are three necessary elements within the parable of the *Sower and the Soils* that must come together before a sinner can be brought to the conviction of sin, understanding the Gospel, and be "born again" . . . "by grace through faith."

1. The "seed" is the Gospel of Jesus Christ with the specific and objective facts **detailing what Christ has accomplished** for sinners through His death, burial, and resurrection/glorification. The sinner MUST understand these specific objective facts.
2. The "Sower" is the Holy Spirit of God who works to illuminate the Gospel to the sinner's heart. The Holy Spirit works in partnership with the Spirit-filled Evangelist as he preaches and explains the details of the Gospel. Although this can happen as the sinner *reads* the Scriptures as well.
3. The various "soils" are the *conditions of the heart* in which various individuals receive the "seed" and respond to the illumination of the Holy Spirit. Therefore the "soils" are primarily the various *conditions of the hearts* (in the *heart's* relationship to various worldly influences) of those to whom the *seed* is being sown. Only genuine repentance can *prepare* the heart for *conversion.*

It is important here to clarify that neither those believing in eternal security, nor those that believe a person can lose his salvation, believe that a person living in habitually sin without evident chastisement from God can say with assurance that they are "born again." The issue is that those believing in eternal security say such living evidences that genuine repentance does not exist and therefore the person had a false profession. Those rejecting eternal security believe such a person was saved, but has lost his salvation. The discussion then should be about deciding which position is supported by the parable of the *soils and the sower.* Exegesis of the text supports that all but one situation results in a false profession as evidenced by individuals failing to continue to grow to the kind of full maturity that produces spiritual fruit.

These first twenty-three verses of Matthew chapter thirteen are addressed primarily to Jewish people (although applicable to all people). It is important to see that this text is dealing with the transition from the Dispensation of Law (Mosaic Covenant) to the Dispensation of Grace (the Church Age). There are some unique conditions here that apply *only in principle* to modern day circumstances.

A key word in the explanation of the parable (verses 18-23) is the word "understandeth." The word "understandeth" is from the Greek word *suniemi* (soon-ee'-ay-mee). The simplest definition is *to put the pieces together*. The idea behind this is the *mental comprehension* of all the details of the Gospel in the supernatural production of faith in the sinner's life leading to complete spiritual understanding of both the *consequences* of unbelief and the *benefits* of saving faith (which is *regeneration*).

Until this *understanding* of the Gospel is accomplished through *illumination* by the Holy Spirit by the careful presentation of the details of the Gospel message, there will never be a proper response to the Gospel, and *conversion in the heart* resulting from a faith decision can never take place (Matthew 13:15; inward transformation; regeneration). **The critical detail here is that *understanding with the head* must become *understanding with the heart* before saving faith is produced through the operations of the Holy Spirit of God (i.e., germination of the seed or regeneration).** The proper response to the Gospel is what defines *believing*, or what is more commonly referred to as *saving faith*. Therefore, true biblical repentance is essential to *preparing the heart for conversion*.

The dilemma of a shallow presentation of the Gospel and various levels of reduction regarding the five Bible verbs that reflect a biblical response to the Gospel will result in innumerable false professions without real *in the heart* conversion. These false professions will produce people who will not be faithful to living for Christ. They may attend church services faithfully, tithe and give faithfully, even live relatively moral lives. However, they were never really saved because they were not *converted in their hearts*. Therefore, they cannot lose a salvation they never had.

There is a deep, unsettling *shallowness* within much of professing Christianity. The depth of this *shallowness* goes much farther than the mere ignorance of the Word of God and apathy towards the things of God. This ignorance of the Word of God and apathy towards the things of God manifested in this *shallowness* are merely symptoms of a much more serious spiritual problem. That problem is self-deception resulting in *pseudo conversions* and *false professions* of faith in Christ. The primary reason for this *shallowness* is the reality that many people have prayed a prayer, walked an aisle, and been *dunked in some water* when in reality they are still lost in trespasses and sin. The problem is a false sense of conversion because there was no real *heartfelt* spiritual conviction of sin and *conversion in the heart*. Understanding with the heart is spiritual *conversion of the heart*.

The Word of God repeatedly addresses the failure of people to be genuinely converted because they do not *understand with their hearts*. *Understanding with the heart* is a strange phrase to us because culturally we have come to think in terms of *understanding with our minds*. The use of the word "heart" in the Bible in ancient times is different than our understanding in modern times. According to the Bible, the *heart* is the central organ of the body, not the *mind*. The *heart* feeds every other organ in the Bible, therefore the condition of the *heart* is preeminent to the body, which is the rest of the organs. We now know that the heart feeds the mind electrolytes through blood supply. These electrolytes determine proper brain function. The point is that God understands all of this because He created the body. God therefore refers to the center of all of man's decisions being *from the heart*, not the brain.

> 'Heart' (Hebrew lebab/leb [b'bel], Gk. Kardia [kardiva]) occurs over one thousand times in the Bible, making it the most common anthropological term in the Scripture. It denotes a person's center for both physical and emotional-intellectual-moral activities; sometimes it is used figuratively for any inaccessible thing.
> The Heart as Center of Physical Activity. 'Heart' denotes to both ancient and modern peoples the beating chest organ protected by the rib cage. Ancient people, however, understood the heart's physical function differently than moderns. From their viewpoint the heart was the central

organ that moved the rest of the body. Ancients ate to strengthen the heart and so revive the body. Abraham offers his weary guests food so that they might 'sustain their hearts' and then go on their way (Gen 18:5). Since moderns understand the anatomy differently than the ancients, the English versions gloss the Hebrew to accommodate it to a more scientific viewpoint.[7]

The point in all of this is that in genuine salvation the heart is *converted.* The Greek word translated "converted" in Matthew 13:15 is *epistrepho* (ep-ee-stref'-o). The meaning is reverted. The idea is that the heart as the center of the physical, emotional, and intellectual is completely *turned around.* If this has not happened, as evidenced by a change in the way a person *feels* about sin and God, *thinks* about sin and God, and *acts* about sin and God, the heart has not been *converted.* God speaks of the unconverted heart of lost Jews as being *hardened* or *stony* (Ezekiel 11:19, 18:31, and 36:26).

> [14] Again the word of the LORD came unto me, saying, [15] Son
> of man, thy brethren, *even* thy brethren, the men of thy
> kindred, and all the house of Israel wholly, *are* they unto
> whom the inhabitants of Jerusalem have said, Get you far
> from the LORD: unto us is this land given in possession. [16]
> Therefore say, Thus saith the Lord GOD; Although I have
> cast them far off among the heathen, and although I have
> scattered them among the countries, yet will I be to them as
> a little sanctuary in the countries where they shall come. [17]
> Therefore say, Thus saith the Lord GOD; I will even gather
> you from the people, and assemble you out of the countries
> where ye have been scattered, and I will give you the land of
> Israel. [18] And they shall come thither, and they shall take
> away all the detestable things thereof and all the
> abominations thereof from thence. [19] <u>And I will give them</u>
> <u>one heart, and I will put a new spirit within you; and I will</u>

[7] Walter A. Edwell, ed., <u>Baker's Evangelical Dictionary of Biblical Theology</u> (Ada:Baker Oublishing Group, 2001), http://www.biblestudytools.com/dictionary/heart/. accessed May19, 2015).

> take the stony heart out of their flesh, and will give them an heart of flesh: 20 **That they** may walk in my statutes, and keep mine ordinances, and do them: and they shall be my people, and I will be their God. 21 But *as for them* whose heart walketh after the heart of their detestable things and their abominations, I will recompense their way upon their own heads, saith the Lord GOD (Ezekiel 11:14-21).

This problem of *pseudo faith* and *false professions* is not new to the Church Age. It has been a problem that is the distinguishing characteristic of failure at the end of every dispensation of God. Each Dispensation ends with the transitioning of God's people from *low expectations* to *no expectations*. This is what ultimately defines apostasy resulting in the reprobation of succeeding generations of people who call themselves children of God without any real conviction of sin, no connection to His expectations of how they live, or having owned the responsibilities that belong to those who have been redeemed.

We fine this to be true at both the endings of the Dispensation of the Law and the Dispensation of Church Age. We find this to be a spiritual constant throughout Scriptures of the *dynamic of apostasy* as Christ answers the question why He spoke in parables. We also find it is this same *dynamic of apostasy* that will exist at the end of the Church Age with the "lukewarm" apostate church of Laodicea. In both cases, we see some readily recognizable characteristics of apostasy.

> 10 And the disciples came, and said unto him, Why speakest thou unto them in parables? 11 He answered and said unto them, Because it is given unto you to know the mysteries of the kingdom of heaven, but to them {*those who had rejected the Gospel in the Law and apostated themselves*} it is not given. 12 For whosoever hath, to him shall be given, and he shall have more abundance: but whosoever hath not, from him shall be taken away even that he hath. 13 Therefore speak I to them in parables: because they seeing see not; and hearing they hear not, neither do they understand. 14 And in them is fulfilled the prophecy of Esaias, which saith, By hearing ye shall hear, and shall not understand; and seeing

ye shall see, and shall not perceive: 15 For this people's **heart is waxed gross**, and *their* **ears are dull of hearing**, and their **eyes they have closed**; lest at any time they should see with *their* eyes, and hear with *their* ears, and should understand with *their* heart, and should be converted, and I should heal them. 16 But blessed *are* your eyes, for they see: and your ears, for they hear. 17 For verily I say unto you, That many prophets and righteous *men* have desired to see *those things* which ye see, and have not seen *them*; and to hear *those things* which ye hear, and have not heard *them* (Matthew 13:10-17).

14 And unto the angel {*messenger* or *pastor*} of the church of the Laodiceans write; These things saith the Amen, the faithful and true witness, the beginning of the creation of God; 15 I know thy works, that thou art neither cold nor hot: I would thou wert cold or hot. 16 So then because thou art lukewarm, and neither cold nor hot, I will spue thee out of my mouth. 17 Because thou sayest, I am rich, and increased with goods, and have need of nothing; and knowest not that thou art wretched, and miserable, and poor, and blind, and naked: 18 I counsel thee to buy of me gold tried in the fire, that thou mayest be rich; and white raiment, that thou mayest be clothed, and ***that* the shame of thy nakedness do not appear**; and anoint thine eyes with eyesalve, that thou mayest see. 19 As many as I love, I rebuke and chasten: be zealous therefore, and repent. 20 Behold, I stand at the door, and knock: if any man hear my voice, and open the door, I will come in to him, and will sup with him, and he with me. 21 To him that overcometh will I grant to sit with me in my throne, even as I also overcame, and am set down with my Father in his throne. 22 He that hath an ear, let him hear what the Spirit saith unto the churches (Revelation 3:14-22).

Questions for Discussion

1. Discuss why it is critically important to know the difference between discussing *assurance of salvation* and teaching *eternal security* to someone showing evidence of a false salvation.

2. Define and discuss the two *straw men* from which the false arguments between Calvinistic eternal security and the Arminian position that says salvation can be lost.

3. Define and discuss the *four operations* of the Spirit of that happen the moment a person is "born again" of the Spirit of God and how these *operations* connect the believer to a new and irreversible *position* "in Christ."

4. List and discuss the three necessary elements within the parable of the *Sower and the Soils* that must come together before a sinner can be brought to the conviction of sin, understanding the Gospel, and being "born again."

5. Thoroughly discuss the differences and what it means to *believe with the heart* as opposed to *believing with the head.*

Chapter Twelve

Propping Up False Conversions

There is an obvious pattern that we can see in Matthew 13:10-17 and Revelation 3:14-22 defining the primary condition of professing believers who are false believers at the end of these two Dispensations. Conversion of the heart is the necessary foundation to *being* a *new creation.* A person cannot be "born again" without getting a new heart that is indwelt by the Person of the Holy Spirit of God. **The potential for spiritual depth lies solely in the conversion of the heart.**

> [10] And the disciples came, and said unto him, Why speakest
> thou unto them in parables? [11] He answered and said unto
> them, Because it is given unto you to know the mysteries of
> the kingdom of heaven, but to them it is not given. [12] For
> whosoever hath, to him shall be given {*the rich are given
> gifts so as to gain their favors*}, and he shall have more
> abundance: but whosoever hath not, from him shall be taken
> away even that he hath {*the poor are often taken advantage
> of because they have no influence with those with power*}. [13]
> Therefore speak I to them in parables {*those apostate and
> corrupted by the injustice of power*}: because they seeing see
> not; and hearing they hear not, neither do they understand. [14]
> And in them is fulfilled the prophecy of Esaias, which saith,
> By hearing ye shall hear, and shall not understand; and
> seeing ye shall see, and shall not perceive: [15] For this
> people's heart is waxed gross, and *their* ears are dull of
> hearing, and their eyes they have closed; lest at any time they
> should see with *their* eyes, and hear with *their* ears, and
> should understand with *their* heart, and should be converted,
> and I should heal them. [16] But blessed *are* your eyes, for they
> see: and your ears, for they hear. [17] For verily I say unto you,
> That many prophets and righteous *men* have desired to see
> *those things* which ye see, and have not seen *them*; and to
> hear *those things* which ye hear, and have not heard *them*
> (Matthew 13:10-17).

The reason that the *shallowness* that manifests false professions continues to go on unchecked is primarily the fault of well-meaning preachers who tend to *prop up* the people living obviously shallow lives. They do this by giving them a false assurance of salvation by teaching them the doctrine of eternal security when they should be teaching them to "Examine yourselves, whether ye be in the faith; prove your own selves. Know ye not your own selves, how that Jesus Christ is in you, except ye be reprobates (II Corinthians 13:5)? Every dispensation of God seems to end with the leaders of God's people progressively lowering God's standards of separation and holiness, allowing for ever decreasing expectations of those who dare call themselves *children of God.*

This is clearly what the Apostle John addresses in his first epistle. By inspiration of the Holy Spirit, John gives a number of *ultimatums* about the reality of a person's profession of faith and the resulting regeneration. These statements of the Apostle John are not intended to add Moralism or Ritualism to the requirements for salvation. These statements of the Apostle John are intended to provide us with spiritual evidences of the manifestation of the indwelling Holy Spirit and evidences of a *new* and *converted heart.* Genuinely "born again" people should *hunger* for genuine "fellowship" with God and other genuine believers.

The central purpose of the first Epistle of John is to establish the criteria to "assure our hearts before" Christ (I John 3:19). The word "assure" in I John 3:19 is from the Greek word *peitho* (pi'-tho). The meaning of the phrase *is convincing through the discovery and presentation of evidence providing an inward certainty* that a person has been "born again" and *converted in his heart.*

The first chapter of I John establishes a governing principle defining a person with a converted heart. A person with a converted heart will long to have fellowship with God. The person with a converted heart understands that although the penalty for all his sin has been remitted "by grace" and "through faith" in the "finished" cross-work of Jesus Christ, that the believer's sin nature remains and he becomes very conscious and convicted of sin in his life. To such a person, I John chapter one is one of the most important chapters of Scripture in the Bible, because I John chapter one tells that person how to restore "fellowship" with God. If "fellowship" with God is not the regular experience of a believer that person is either ignorant of I John Chapter one or is not converted in his heart. The indwelling Spirit of God is literarily the "mind of Christ" and the heart of God joined together with the heart and mind of the believer. This reality is what defines a *converted heart*. This reality is what generates the believer being a *New Creation* (II Corinthians 5:17).

Although the subject matter of I John 1:5-10 is about "fellowship" with God, the text also defines the parameters for biblical separation. There is an area in the transition from *light* to *darkness* that is apparent. Although there is also a transition area between *light* and *darkness* where vision is not clear, it is clear that this transition area is borderline and questionable as to the dominance of either *light* or *darkness*. In the application of the metaphor to "walk in the light," it is clearly referring to the area where the *light* is dominant.

The wise and genuine believer will not hesitate to avoid the *transitional area* rather than risk breaking his "fellowship" with God. The person with a new and converted heart considers God's will before his own will in any matter. The wise believer would not risk his taking liberty in questionable areas of truth. If there are areas he views as questionable, he flees back into the *light* rather than taking liberty to walk in areas of which he is unsure of God's will in a matter.

> 5 This then is the message which we have heard of him, and
> declare unto you, that God is light, and in him is no darkness
> at all. 6 If we say that we have fellowship with him, and walk
> in darkness, we lie, and do not the truth: 7 But if we walk in
> the light, as he is in the light, we have fellowship one with
> another, and the blood of Jesus Christ his Son cleanseth us
> from all sin. 8 If we say that we have no sin, we deceive
> ourselves, and the truth is not in us. 9 If we confess our sins,
> he is faithful and just to forgive us *our* sins, and to cleanse
> us from all unrighteousness. 10 If we say that we have not
> sinned, we make him a liar, and his word is not in us (I John
> 1:5-10).

I John 1:8 is important in the context of I John chapter one. The verse makes an emphatic point to the juxtaposition between having been "born again" into the New Creation with the fact that all believers still possess a sin nature and are still part of the fallen creation. The point of I John 1:8 is that all saints are still sinners. They still exist within the fallen creation because they are not yet glorified. Therefore, if we somehow think we are no longer sinners just because we have been "born again" and have a *new heart*, we will miss the point of the necessity in making personal choices about where we walk and how we live. The point is that we will fail God by occasionally making sinful and selfish choices. When that happens, the truly "born again" person will quickly recognize his sin before God, repent, confess that sin, and quickly return to the "light" of living in "fellowship" with God. The truly "born again" person will be convicted of sin in any form in his life (*sinful acts, thoughts, or emotions*) and will not be able to enjoy *walking in darkness*.

Think of the imagery intended by the metaphors of *walking in darkness* and *walking in light*. What thoughts would have entered the minds of people two thousand years ago when these metaphors were used? These people would have thought of the daytime and the natural light from the Sun. They would have thought of the darkness of night. Law abiding people were usually in their homes by sundown. It was very dangerous to go outside after the darkness of nightfall. People looked very suspiciously upon anyone outside their homes after nightfall. The darkness was the realm of unrighteousness. Wild animals and criminals lurked in the darkness. Most homes would keep a lamp lit in the window during the night. Outside the cities, flickering campfires would light the night sky keeping thieves and wild animals at a safe distance. Watchmen were posted to guard against intruders.

At the time of the writing of I John, "light" and "darkness" carried considerably more relevant meaning than they do to us of the *Age of Electricity* and light at the *flick of a switch.* When nightfall came and darkness engulfed their lives, these people made sure they were prepared by lighting fires and burning lamps. Walking in the darkness was not only very dangerous; most people considered going into the darkness very foolish. Staying in the light provided a person with a *circle of security.* This is the context of the metaphors.

The word "walk" in I John 1:6 and 7 is translated from the Greek word *peripateo* (per-ee-pat-eh'-o). The word means to *tread all around.* The idea is to *live in a companion existence.* There is the implication of becoming *comfortable in the darkness or light.* The word "walk" carries the same meaning about both "the darkness" and "the light." The truly "born again" person will never be comfortable walking in the darkness or living in the pleasures of sin.

It is important for believers to understand this meaning because to "walk in darkness" breaks "fellowship" with God. To "walk in the light" brings the believer into "fellowship" with God. The "darkness" implies unrighteousness. The "light" implies righteousness. The "darkness" implies failure to be separated from worldliness in unrighteousness. The "light" implies separation from worldliness and unto righteousness. The word "walk" implies the common place of existence where a person has become comfortable. No one has a biblical right to become comfortable with anything that is unrighteous. All false doctrine is unrighteous. To become comfortable with walking in false doctrine and failure to be separate from unrighteousness is to become content with living outside of "fellowship" with God.

The broad meaning of "light" is right doctrine (orthodoxy). The meaning then of *walking in the light* is the right practice of right doctrine (orthopraxy). Therefore, *walking in the light* is having right doctrine that results in righteous living. In this context of right doctrine resulting in righteous living, there MUST BE the absence of worldliness (I John 2:15). To profess correct doctrine while using worldly, sensual music to worship God is a contradiction against right doctrine. Right doctrine would not allow the use of worldly, sensual music to worship God. Worldly music for worship is *Neo-paganism*.

For instance, *toleration* of Calvin's views of the doctrine of salvation (Soteriology) is a contradiction against orthopraxy. Calvin's views of the doctrine of salvation corrupt Theology in the biblical view of the love of God (John 3:16). Monergism corrupts how God's saves "by grace through faith" (Ephesians 2:8-9). The corrupt belief about *sovereign election* of who can be saved corrupts how God uses the human agent in evangelism (Romans 10:14-15). The corrupt belief about *sovereign election* of who can be saved as well corrupts the Bible teaching about the universal availability of salvation to "whosever will" (Romans 10:13). One cannot "walk in the light" and be tolerant of either false doctrine (heterodoxy) or unrighteous practices (heteropraxy). In fact, to be tolerant of either false doctrine (heterodoxy) or unrighteous practices (heteropraxy) is to *walk in darkness*. This person cannot have "fellowship" with God until he repents of his heterodoxy and heteropraxy. In other words, to have "fellowship" with God, he must turn away from his false doctrine and cease tolerating and participating in false practices.

In many cases, people want to emphasize *walking in the light* while ignoring the admonition to not "walk in darkness." To do so is to completely distort I John 1:5-9. Both *walking in the light* and not *walking in the darkness* need to be emphasized equally. To *walk in the light*, a person CANNOT be *walking in darkness*. A person that is *walking in darkness* CANNOT be *walking in the light*. The practical significance of this is the practical absolutes necessary to live in a *working partnership* ("fellowship") with God. *Walking in the light* and not *walking in darkness* are equally important.

Another paradigm shift in the evolution of the "lukewarm" church is the de-emphasizing of doctrine to maximize spiritual *unity*. A simple precursory evaluation of such a statement ought to immediately reveal the paradox to I John 1:5-9. Spiritual *unity* cannot exist apart from doctrinal *unity*, because doctrine always affects practice. To minimize doctrine is a complete contradiction against the biblical instruction to *walk in the light*. Ignorance of Bible doctrine is *darkness*. Unrighteousness is *walking in the darkness* of that ignorance. False teachers depend upon doctrinal ignorance to make merchandise of people that come under their leadership.

> [5] This then is the message which we have heard of him, and declare unto you, that God is light, and in him is no darkness at all. [6] If we say that we have fellowship with him, and walk in darkness, we lie, and do not the truth: [7] But if we walk in the light, as he is in the light, we have fellowship one with another, and the blood of Jesus Christ his Son cleanseth us from all sin (I John 1:5-7).

I John 1:5-7 is a remarkably definitive statement establishing exact boundaries for "fellowship" with God. These few verses also establish exact doctrinal perimeters for personal and Ecclesiastical separation. "God is light, and in him is no darkness at all." There is clear, visible division between darkness and light. It is apparent where light ends and darkness begins.

The definitive factor here is between people either following a *fallen heart* or following their *new heart*. I have spent a lifetime trying to help people who *follow their fallen heart*. A fallen heart is "deceitful above all things and desperately wicked" (Jerimiah 17:9). Following a fallen heart will always eventually lead you into darkness. You cannot trust a fallen heart. You cannot trust a fallen heart to choose a husband or wife. You cannot trust a fallen heart to make any kind of righteous life choices. You need a new heart that habitually yielded to the indwelling Spirit of God. False professions create a façade of spirituality without the spiritual power that genuinely produces true Bible defined righteousness.

Light is the glory of God. Light is the revelation of God in all His wondrous attributes. To "walk in the light, as He is in the light" is to live the communicable attributes of God through the supernatural enabling of the filling of the Holy Spirit. This defines glorifying God. The light is manifested by the "fruit of the Spirit" and God is revealed through the believer's life. Walking in the light is defined in extreme detail in Ephesians chapters five and six along with Galatians chapter five. We notice that in both statements there is an emphasis upon righteousness and separation from **all false doctrine and sinful practices**. God is de-glorified through compromising doctrinal purity or calling unrighteousness righteousness. The Epistle to the church at Ephesus makes the same kind of statements.

Although there was a large contingency of Jews at Ephesus, they lived in a culture consumed by paganism. The Temple of Diana was at Ephesus. The clear majority of the converts in the church at Ephesus were saved pagans. Although the believers at Ephesus were doing better in their issues of living for the Lord than those at Corinth, Paul still addresses the influences and practices of the carnal paganism at Ephesus. In Ephesians 5:3, Paul addresses the reality that true "saints" should be identifiable by a *new lifestyle* that corresponds with a *new heart*. This is an expansion upon his earlier statement in Ephesians 2:8-10. Usually the emphasis is put upon Ephesians 2:8-9. However, the context puts the emphasis on Ephesians 2:10.

> [4] But God, who is rich in mercy, for his great love wherewith
> he loved us, [5] Even when we were dead in sins, hath
> quickened us together with Christ, (by grace ye are saved;)
> {*perfect, passive, participle*} [6] And hath raised *us* up
> together, and made *us* sit together in heavenly *places* in
> Christ Jesus: [7] That in the ages to come he might shew the
> exceeding riches of his grace in *his* kindness toward us
> through Christ Jesus. [8] For by grace are ye saved {*perfect,
> passive, participle*} through faith; and that not of yourselves:
> *it is* the gift of God: [9] Not of works, lest any man should
> boast. [10] For we are his workmanship, created in Christ Jesus
> unto good works, which God hath before ordained that we
> should walk in them. [11] Wherefore remember, that ye *being*
> in time past Gentiles in the flesh, who are called
> Uncircumcision by that which is called the Circumcision in
> the flesh made by hands; [12] That at that time ye were without
> Christ, being aliens from the commonwealth of Israel, and
> strangers from the covenants of promise, having no hope,
> and without God in the world: [13] But now in Christ Jesus ye

who sometimes were far off are made nigh by the blood of Christ (Ephesians 2:4-13).

The context of a radically new life flowing from a converted new heart in the statement of Ephesians 2:10 then carries throughout the rest of the epistle. The context is the priesthood of all believers ministering before God and to the world. Continue this context into the statements in Ephesians 5:3-21.

> 3 But fornication, and all uncleanness, or covetousness, let it not be once named among you {*the implication appears to be never allowing these practices to be connected to your name or testimony-either individually or as a local church*}, as becometh {*suitable, proper, in that such practices do not fit the idea of being*} saints {*sanctified and separated ones*}; 4 Neither filthiness {*obscenity*}, nor foolish talking {*gross, course, crude, and uneducated talk*} , nor jesting {*without moral character controls*}, which are not convenient {*fitting to saints*}: but rather giving of thanks. 5 For this ye know, that no whoremonger, nor unclean person, nor covetous man, who is an idolater, hath any inheritance in the kingdom of Christ and of God. 6 Let no man deceive you with vain words: for because of these things cometh the wrath of God upon the children of disobedience. 7 Be not ye therefore partakers {*co-participants in their disobedience*} with them. 8 For ye **were** sometimes darkness, but **now** *are ye* light in the Lord: **walk as children of light**: 9 (For the fruit of the Spirit *is* in all **goodness** and **righteousness** and **truth**;) 10 Proving {*testing or being discerning of all teachings and associations in order to approve*} what is acceptable unto the Lord. 11 And have no fellowship {*sugkoinoneo – co-participation*} with the unfruitful works of darkness, but rather reprove *them {the meaning is to convince or convict them of their error}*. 12 For it is a shame even to speak of those things which are done of them in secret. . 13 But all things {*unscriptural*} that are reproved {*addressed by Scriptural correction*} are made manifest {*exposed*} by the light {*Scripture Truth*}: for whatsoever doth make manifest {*exposes as sin and/or error*} is light {*the light exposes what*

is hidden in the darkness}. 14 Wherefore he saith, Awake
thou that sleepest, and arise from the dead, and Christ shall
give thee light *{referring to the illumination of the
indwelling Holy Spirit providing the Spirit-filled believer
with spiritual discernment}*. 15 See then that ye walk
circumspectly *{with exactness or perfectly straight}*, not as
fools, but as wise, 16 Redeeming *{rescue from waste}* the
time, because the days *{as the continuum of time}* are evil
{in affect or influence}. 17 Wherefore be ye not unwise
{mindless, stupid, ignorant}, but understanding *{put
together to mentally comprehend}* what the will of the Lord
is. 18 And be not drunk with wine *{and thereby controlled or
influenced by it; drunkenness was a common part of the
pagan worship at Ephesus – their **Bacchanalia** or feasts
dedicated to Bacchus, the god of wine}*, wherein is excess
{asotia, which literally means unsavedness}; but be filled
{crammed full} with the Spirit; 19 Speaking to yourselves in
psalms and hymns and spiritual songs *{The **Bacchanalia**
were preoccupied with lurid, sensual songs intended to
entice and seduce into licentious practices. Christians
should be preoccupied with spiritual songs about God.}*,
singing and making melody in your heart to the Lord; 20
Giving thanks always for all things unto God and the Father
in the name of our Lord Jesus Christ; 21 Submitting
yourselves one to another in the fear of God (Ephesians 5:3-
21).

Obviously, Ephesians chapter five is an important portion of Scripture to help us understand what it means to "walk in the light, as He is in the light" (I John 1:7). As a believer walks "in the light, as He is in the light," he has entered into "fellowship" with God and the Spirit of God produces the "fruit of the Spirit" through that believer's life/walk. Through the "fruit of the Spirit," the believer himself becomes *light* and thereby glorifies God.

Questions for Discussion

1. Discuss the defining factor given in the first chapter of the epistle of I John that manifests a person with a *converted heart*.

2. Although most professing Christians are content with living in the transitional area between *darkness* and *light*, discuss what God means when He demands that believers "walk in the light" before He will have *fellowship* with them.

3. Discuss and explain what it means and what is involved in walking "in the light."

4. Discuss and explain what it means and what is involved in walking "in darkness."

5. Discuss the significance of the two uses of the word "saved" in Ephesians 2:5 and Ephesians 2:8 being in the perfect tense, passive voice, and participle mood and how this requires an understanding that **IF** a person is "born again," this *new creation* is *once and forever*.

Bibliography

The books listed in this Bibliography have contributed in various ways to the content of ***Learning to Lead***. However, not every book is quoted in this book or noted in the footnotes. The author is grateful for the contributions of many great men noted in this Bibliography whose writings have touched upon the doctrine of salvation. The author of this book does not agree with everything these men have written or with all their conclusions.

Alford, Henry. ***Alford's Greek Testament, Volumes I through IV.*** Grand Rapids, Michigan: Baker Book House, 1980.

Anderson, Neil T. ***The Bondage Breaker: Overcoming Negative Thought, Irrational Feelings, & Habitual Sins.*** Eugene, Oregon: Harvest House Publishers, 1980.

Angus, S. ***The Mystery Religions.*** New York: Dover Publications, 1975.

Barbieri, Louis A. ***First and Second Peter.*** Chicago: Moody Press, 1979.

Barnes, Albert. ***Revelation; Barnes' Notes on the New Testament, Volumes one through twenty-seven.*** Grand Rapids: Baker Book House, 1981.

Binney, Jim. ***Living Purely in an Impure World.*** New Concord: The Counselor's Pen Publications, 2003.

Boer, Harry R. ***A Short History of the Early Church.*** Grand Rapids: Wm. B. Eerdmans Pub. Co., April 1981.

Boice, James Montgomery. ***The Minor Prophets.*** Grand Rapids: Zondervon Publishing House, 1986.

Bruce, A. B. ***The Training of the Twelve.*** Grand Rapids: Kregal Publications, 1978.

Bruce, E.F. ***The Epistles of John.*** Grand Rapids: Wm. B. Eerdmans Pub. Co., 1979.

Bruce, E.F. ***The Hard Sayings of Jesus.*** Downers Grove: InterVarsity Press, 1983.

Bruce, E.F. ***What the Bible Teaches About What Jesus Did.*** Wheaton: Tyndale House Publishers, Inc., 1979.

Bullinger, E.W. ***Number In Scripture.*** Grand Rapids: Kregal Publications, 1980.

Chafer, Lewis Sperry. ***Systematic Theology, Volumes I through VII***. Dallas: Dallas Seminary Press, Thirteenth Printing, June, 1976.

Couch, Mal, Editor. ***A Bible Handbook to the Acts of the Apostles.*** Grand Rapids: Kregel Publications, 1999.

Crow, Paul. ***Cliffs and Fences.*** Kings Mountain: Evangelist Paul Crow Ministries, 2008.

Dehaan, M. R. ***Studies in First Corinthians.*** Grand Rapids: Zondervon Publishing House, 1981.

Delany, James. ***Abiding In Christ: God's Plan for Spiritual Growth.*** Salem: James Delany, 2000.

Farrell, Tom. ***Preaching That Pleases God.*** Lancaster: Striving Together Publications, 2010.

Gaebelein, Frank E. ***The Expositor's Bible Commentary, Volume 11.*** Grand Rapids: Zondervon Publishing House, 1981.

Garraty, John A. and Gay, Peter, eds., ***The Columbia History of the World.*** New York: Harper and Row Publishers, 1981.

Getz, Gene A. ***The Measure of a Church.*** Glendale: G.L. Regal Books, 1979.

Getz, Gene A. ***Sharpening the Focus of the Church.*** Chicago: Moody Press, 1974.

Green, Michael. ***Evangelism in the Early Church.*** Grand Rapids: Wm. B. Eerdmans Pub. Co., 1985.

Hengstenberg, E. W. ***Christology of the Old Testament and a Commentary on Messianic Predictions.*** Grand Rapids: Kregel Publications, 1976.

Hunt, Dave and McMahon, T.A. ***The Seduction of Christianity.*** Eugene: Harvest House Publishers, 1986.

Jackson, Jeremy C. ***No Other Foundation, The Church Through Twenty Centuries.*** Cornerstone Books, 1980.

Jamieson-Fausset-Brown Commentary; Sword Searcher Software, CD-ROM, version 6.1.1.3. Broken Arrow, OK, 1995-2011 StudyLamp Software LLC.

Jenson, Ron and Steven, Jim. ***Dynamics of Church Growth.*** Grand Rapids: Baker Bookhouse, 1981.

Keddie, Gordon J. ***Looking For the Good Life: The Search for Fulfillment in the Light of Ecclesiastes.*** Phillipsburg: Presbyterian and Reformed Publishing Co., 1991.

Kidner, Derek. ***The Wisdom of Proverbs, Job, & Ecclesiastes.*** Downers Grove: InterVarsity Press, 1985.

Kistemaker, Simon J. ***New Testament Commentary: Acts.*** Grand Rapids: Baker Book House Co., 1990.

Kuen, Alfred F. ***I Will Build My Church.*** Chicago: Moody Press, Translated from original French Edition in 1971.

Lightfoot, J.B. (and Harner, J.R.) ***The Apostolic Fathers (Second Edition).*** Grand Rapids: Baker Book House Co., 1990.

MacArthur, John. ***God, Satan and Angels.*** Chicago: Moody Press, 1993.

MacArthur, John. ***The Charismatics.*** Grand Rapids: Zondervan Publishing House, 1980.

MacArthur, John. ***Body Dynamics.*** Wheaton: Victor Books, 1982.

Machen, J. Gresham. ***The Origen of Paul's Religion.*** Grand Rapids: Wm. B. Eerdmans Pub. Co., 1921.

Mack, Michael C. ***The Synergy Church: A Strategy for Integrating Small Groups and Sunday School.*** Grand Rapids: Baker Book House Co., 1996.

Maynard, Michael. M.L.S.; ***A History of the Debate Over I John 5:7-8***. Tempe: Comma Publications, 1995.

Matteson, Earle E. ***The Biblical Plan For Power.*** Lakewood: Matteson Ministries, 1989.

Matthew Poole's Commentary on the Whole Bible; Sword Searcher Software, CD-ROM, version 6.1.1.3. Broken Arrow, OK, 1995-2011 StudyLamp Software LLC.

Moffatt, James. ***The Expositor's Greek Testament, ed. by W. R. Nicoll, Volumes I through IV.*** Grand Rapids: Wm. B. Eerdmans Publishing Co., 1980.

Morgan, G. Campbell. ***The Acts of the Apostles.*** New York: Fleming H. Revell Co., 1924.

Morris, Leon. ***Tyndale New Testament Commentaries, ed. R.V.G. Tasker, Volumes I through XX.*** Grand Rapids: Wm. B. Eerdmans Publishing Co., 1980.

Nash, Ronald H. ***Christian Faith and Historical Understanding.*** Grand Rapids: Zondervan Publishing House, 1984.

Newell, William R., ***Romans Verse by Verse***; SwordSearcher Software, CD-ROM, version 6.1.1.3. Broken Arrow, OK, 1995-2011 StudyLamp Software LLC.

Paige, Richard L. Jr. ***The Church Christ Built.*** Minneapolis: North Star Baptist Press, 1999.

Phillips, John. ***Exploring Acts.*** Neptune: Loizeaux Brothers, 1991.

Radmacher, Earl D. ***What the Church Is All About.*** Chicago: Moody Press, 1978.

Ravenhill, Leonard. ***Why Revival Tarries.*** Minneapolis: Bethany House Publishers, 1983.

Robertson, Archibald T. ***Word Pictures in The New Testament, Volumes I through VI.*** Grand Rapids: Baker Book House, 1933.

Ryrie, Charles Caldwell. ***The Holy Spirit.*** Chicago: Moody Press, 1973.

Saucy, Robert L. ***The Church in God's Program.*** Chicago: Moody Press, 1972.

Saxe, Raymond H. ***The Battle for Your Bible: A Study of Experience Versus Scriptural Tongues.*** Ann Arbor: Grace Bible Publications, 1978.

Schaff, Philip. ***History of the Christian Church (8 Volumes).*** Grand Rapids: Eerdmans Printing Co., 1980.

Scofield, C.I. ***Scofield Reference Bible***. Edited by Rev. C.I. Scofield, Oxford University Press, Inc., New and Improved Edition.

Seibel, Alexander. ***The Church Subtly Deceived?*** (Colombia, South Carolina: The Olive Press, 1996).

Sottau, Henry W. ***The Holy Vessels and Furniture of the Tabernacle.*** Grand Rapids: Kregal Publications, 1975.

Sottau, Henry W. ***The Tabernacle, the Priesthood and the Offerings.*** Grand Rapids: Kregal Publications, 1974.

Stott, John R. W. ***The Message of Ephesians.*** Downers Grove: Inter-Varsity Press, 1979.

Stravinskas, Peter M.J., Editor. ***Our Sunday Visitor's Catholic Encyclopedia.*** Huntington: Our Sunday Visitor Publishing Division, 1991.

Strouse, Thomas M. ***An Exegesis of Psalm 119.*** Newington: Emanuel Baptist Publications, 2008.

Tasker, R.V.G. ***The Gospel of John: Tyndale N.T. Commentaries, Vol. IV.*** Grand Rapids: Wm. B. Eerdman's Printing Company, 1980.

Tenney, Merrill C. ***John: The Gospel of Belief.*** Grand Rapids: Wm. B. Eerdman's Printing Company, 1977.

Thomas, Major W. Ian. ***The Saving Life of Christ.*** Grand Rapids: Zondervon Publishing House, 1961.

Tillapaugh, Frank R. ***Unleashing the Church: Getting People Out of the Fortress and Into Ministry.*** Ventura: Regal Books, 1982.

Thomson, William M. ***The Land and the Book.*** Grand Rapids: Baker Book House Co., 1955.

Thomas, David. ***Acts of the Apostles Expository and Homiletical***. Grand Rapids: Kregel Publications, 1980, Orig. pub. 1870 ed. Published by R.D. Dickinson. Homiletic Commentary on the Acts of the Apostles.

Thomas, David. ***Gospel of John.*** Grand Rapids: Kregel Publications, 198).

Thomas, David. ***Gospel of Matthew: Expository and Homiletical.*** Grand Rapids: Kregel Publications, 1979.

Unger, Merrill F. ***Unger's Survey of the Bible.*** Eugene: Harvest House Publishers, 1985.

Unger, Merrill F. ***The Baptism & Gifts of the Holy Spirit.*** Chicago: Moody Press, 1981.

Unger, Merrill F. ***Zechariah: Prophet of Messiah's Glory.*** Grand Rapids: Zondervon Publishing House, 1982.

Vincent, Marvin R. ***Word Studies in the New Testament, Volumes I through IV.*** Grand Rapids: Wm. B. Eerdman's Publishing Co., 1980.

Walvoord, John F. ***The Holy Spirit at Work Today.*** Chicago: Moody Press, 1973.

Wemp, C. Sumner. ***How on Earth Can I Be Spiritual?*** Nashville: Thomas Nelson, Inc. Publishers, 1978.

Wiersbe, Warren W. ***Be Fruitful: How to be faithful to the Word, your tasks, and the people who need you.*** Wheaton: Victor Books, 1988.

Wood, Leon. ***A Survey of Israel's History.*** Grand Rapids: Zondervon Publishing House, 1978.

Zodhiates, Spiros. ***Getting the Most Out of Life: An Exposition of I Corinthians 3.*** Ridgefield: AMG Publishers, 1976.

Lexicons and Dictionaries

Theological Dictionary of the New Testament, Ten Volumes
Edited by Gerhard Kittel and Gerhard Friedrich. Translated and edited by Geoffrey W. Bromiley.
Wm. B. Eerdmans Publishing Co., reprinted September 1983

Richards, Lawrence O.
Expository Dictionary of Bible Words
Regency Reference Library
Zondervan Publishing House, 1985

Thayer, Joseph H.
Thayer's Greek English Lexicon of the New Testament
Baker Book House, Fifth Printing March 1980

Unger, Merrill F.
The New Unger's Bible Dictionary
Edited by R.K. Harrison, Howard F. Vos and Cyril J. Barber contributing editors.
Moody Press, Revised and updated 1988

Vine, W. E.
An Expository Dictionary of New Testament Words
Fleming H. Revell Company, Seventeenth impression, 1966

The Zondervan Pictoral Encyclopedia of the Bible, Five Volumes
General Editor: Merrill C. Tenney
Associate Editor: Steven Barabas
Zondervan Publishing House; Fifth Printing 1982

www.ingramcontent.com/pod-product-compliance
Lightning Source LLC
Chambersburg PA
CBHW052007090426
42741CB00008B/1587